P. 71-Mindse...
P. 72. Be da...
P. 77- Wild...
P 84- Prove yourself you can do it

# JOHN
# WILLKOM

Rebounding- P 89 - put the wooden them.

John Willkom is a former Division 1 basketball player at Marquette University, who later earned his MBA from Loyola University Chicago. The co-founder of Playmakers Basketball, John implemented collegiate-level workouts into a basketball camp circuit and AAU program aimed to provide better opportunities to kids in the Midwest. Prior to his current role as an ecommerce executive, John worked with high school and collegiate athletic programs on the importance of proper nutrition and the development of fueling stations to enhance athletic performance. Widely recognized for his basketball passion, you can still find John coaching youth teams and playing pick-up games at a local gym. John, his wife, Allison, and their daughter, Avery, currently reside in Portland, Oregon, where John serves on the board of Portland State University's Center for Retail Leadership.

Blitz- Defense vs Ballscreen P.95

Defense - get 3 stops in A Row - P/R 125

P.122 - Toughness - maintain )
ask players - how

P.179 you can't be afraid of what your capable of !

To my parents, Monte and Patti,
who encouraged me to chase my dreams.

# WALK-ON WARRIOR

## DRIVE, DISCIPLINE, AND THE WILL TO WIN

By John Willkom

# CONTENTS

# FOREWORD

I was recently asked, "Why would you go back and write a book almost thirteen years after the fact?" That question alone ignited a spark deep within. It was something that had been on my mind for years since college. During my sophomore season of college basketball, I had begun to write down stories, thinking to myself that I couldn't let these moments be forgotten. Maybe one day I would share them with my wife and kids, or maybe they'd just disappear into cyberspace. Writing here and there through college, the stories had begun to pile up, but other things always seemed to take precedence, and the idea of a book being published just wasn't a priority. Fast forward thirteen years, and for whatever reason, I can't seem to live with myself without finishing this book. The funny thing is that the motivation has nothing to do with me, but everything to do with other people. My hope for this book is to inspire, even just one kid, that big things are possible in small towns, and great players are never the ones with the best shoes. Basketball has taken me near and far, but it's not the games I remember. It's the people, the workouts, the love and passion for the game that made individuals so much fun to be around. Chase your dreams, believe in yourself, and enjoy the journey.

I would also like to briefly reflect on the title of this book, *Walk-On Warrior*. Warriors was the proud nickname for Marquette University athletics from 1954-1994, when the mascot was changed to Golden Eagles citing that previous Warriors logos had been offensive to Native Americans. While the Warriors name is no longer officially associated with Marquette athletics, many fans of the program still outwardly reference the nickname. Marquette's first and only men's basketball national championship came in 1977, when the Al McGuire led Warriors defeated the University of North Carolina. Name and logo aside, the Warriors name over the years very much came to embody the tough and resilient style of play that fans and fellow programs came to expect from Marquette. For all the players, fans, and alumni that can relate, this one's for you.

# 1

# COMMITMENT

I'm a 33-year-old white male that's about to board a plane from Portland, OR, to New York City. This isn't a normal route for me, so while I travel a lot, I'm stuck flying Delta with no frequent flyer miles, which consequently sticks me in a middle seat in the second to last row of the aircraft. It's 5:48 a.m., I'm not a coffee drinker, and I swear it's been forty-five minutes since we started boarding. Ain't life great!

A few weeks before this, I had taken another Delta flight, and after reading in the airline magazine that Delta CEO, Ed Bastian, responds to every email he receives, I decided to try my luck. "Hey Ed," I wrote. I proceeded to offer my ideas on how to improve the boarding process, such as boarding from the back to the front with window seats first, then middle, and finally aisle. I also suggested that planes should offer storage bins below the seats instead of above, as there's not a flight without people struggling to get their bags overhead.

Rather than stop there, I threw in another idea for good measure. Every airline needs to change the beverage process. Instead of taking orders, offer everyone a $10 food/drink credit and allow them to eat and drink when they want to.

To Ed's credit, he did respond, at 3:23 a.m. eastern time. "Thanks John. Appreciate your suggestions and your business."

Back to today, I'm flying to the east coast to meet with an important business partner. It's mid-February, which means I'm leaving a rainstorm in Portland for a forecasted snowstorm in New York. Because of my seat position, I was forced to gate check my bag, and I'm told there is absolutely no room for my large, puffy winter jacket in the overhead bins. Hell, I'm in the middle seat of row thirty-three; I might as well burn a few calories while I'm there.

The woman on my left is already chatting, and while I appreciate her friendliness, this conversation won't last more than five minutes because I'm half asleep the moment I sit down. It's hard to sleep on planes, but I'm tired, and the alternative is being acutely aware of my uncomfortableness for five hours. Of course, we take off, and my plan is abruptly aborted as this woman proceeds to crunch through a New York Times, half of the paper strewn across my leg.

When I can't sleep on planes, I do crossword puzzles. I usually get about half way, then end up checking the answers to revitalize my effort. Today's my lucky day, as I'm asked for a four-letter word that describes a "landing place for ships." I take a wild guess and write "Quay," which is not only correct, but reflects more on my memory than my vocabulary, as I could swear I had read that clue before. Regardless, I solve about half the clues, and despite my somewhat consistent practice, I never seem to get any further.

As I shelve the crossword puzzle, I burrow back into my jacket. You know those moments when you're trying to fall asleep, and you think about what it is you want to dream about it? My first thought is the business meeting I'll have later that day. *Am I prepared? What did I miss? Finally, I can't keep thinking about this because I'll never fall asleep!*

But just like that, my mind goes blank. And as I think about nothing, the dream I'm supposed to have just shows up.

# 2

# THE BEGINNING

It's December 1991: Operation Desert Storm is taking place in the Middle East, and there are now one million computers worldwide connected to the internet! But, at the age of seven, I'm neither fighting Saddam or surfing the web. I'm back in St. John's gymnasium in Marshfield, my hometown of 18,800 people, located in the geographic center of Wisconsin. As I walk in, the space is pitch black, and the smell of an "old gym" permeates the air. "Hit the lights," shouts my dad, and for the next five minutes, we wait near the stage while the lamps heat up.

I began playing basketball at an early age, and I learned right away that practice was the only way to separate myself from the other kids. My dad coached an eighth-grade girls team at St. John's, and if I got my homework done, I'd join him at practice so I could hang out in and around the gym. Out of respect for the team and my dad, my presence was welcome anytime, but I had to sit and watch, and no dribbling was allowed during practice. I watched my dad teach the fundamentals, and the girls worked hard but had fun. My dad stressed man to man defense and was a stickler about seeing the basketball and rotating to help on any penetration to the basket. I listened, learned, and admittedly thought to myself, *Some of these girls stink at basketball*. Yet, I respected them because they worked hard, and they played for my dad. When the final whistle would blow to signal the end of practice, I'd grab a ball, sprint onto the floor, and work on my game. Early on, my dad always told me that I needed to be able to dribble and shoot with both hands. We worked on my left hand and shot a lot of left-handed layups. The other thing he stressed was developing good shot form. He frowned whenever I'd shoot three-pointers, and consequently, I worked on being able to make short shots and shoot the way he taught me. When it was time to go, we'd put the balls in the sports closet, which contained junior high football gear, volleyball equipment, and a rack of basketballs. I spent a lot of time in that room trying on old jerseys, football pads, helmets, etc. In fact, my dad actually bought a couple of used helmets, shoulder pads, and football pants from the school one year as a Christmas gift for my brother and me. It was the coolest present I ever received.

My dad was a graduate of Marquette University and was a student during their first and only men's basketball national championship in 1977. If Marquette was playing on TV, my dad would usually have it on, and I remember watching guys like Aaron Hutchins, Damon Key, Tony Miller, Chris Crawford, and Jim McIlvaine. My dad would talk about the legendary Al McGuire and Rick "The Pick" Majerus. We'd watch other college basketball teams as well, but nobody played harder than Marquette according to my dad. Maybe he was a little biased, but they were my team.

Starting in second grade, I attended my first basketball camp with Coach Andy Banasik at Marshfield Columbus High School. Columbus was the local Catholic high school and had a strong athletic tradition. The camp was great: ball handling drills, shooting drills, defense, you name it. We had various contests, and every winner would get a certificate. Camps today seem to focus almost exclusively on offensive skills, but I actually won a "Lane Slides" certificate for doing the most defensive slides, lane line to lane line, in one minute.

Kevin Orr was the junior varsity basketball coach at Columbus at the time and was also my physical education teacher at St. John's elementary school. Orr stood about 5'10", with short, dark hair and an athletic build. Mr. Orr, as I knew him, was a ball full of energy. He came to school every day fired up about something, and I respected him because I knew he coached at Columbus. Mr. Orr would occasionally spit when he talked, which would elicit giggles from the kids sitting Indian style on the gym floor waiting for directions. One day, Mr. Orr announced that we were heading out to the parking lot for gym class. Tag, dodgeball, football? Regardless of your guess, you'd be wrong, as he led us to an open space of blacktop, marked with two cones on each end. Lining us up single file, he told us we'd run, one at a time, from one set of cones to the other. "Wait for the whistle!" he yelled. Each kid had an opportunity to run, while Mr. Orr held a stopwatch and clip board. I was a fast kid, and I probably ran six or seven times because it was fun, not realizing that I was being evaluated on my forty-yard dash time with each blare of the whistle. When the class ended, Orr gathered us around and reminded us to "keep working," which to a group of second-graders didn't mean much of anything.

In all seriousness, I really liked to run, and at the end of the school year, I attended an informational session for the Marshfield Youth Track Club (MYTC). Dr. Garry Martin was a podiatrist in Marshfield and had a passion for track & field. For the next two summers, I went to track practice a couple nights a week during the summer and learned how to high jump, long jump, and throw a discus. We'd warm up with knee highs, butt kicks, cariocas, power skipping, and some short sprints, and we had a diverse group of athletes in all shapes and sizes. I say that because I ran the 200-meter dash with Adam Stenavich, who would later start at left tackle for the Michigan Wolverines and play in the NFL for the Carolina Panthers. Dr. Martin's son, Garry II, was a few years older than me and was a phenomenal athlete. Garry II seemed to excel at everything, including the shot put and discus, and it made sense when he was later awarded a full scholarship to South Carolina as a decathlete.

Most decorated, though, was a kid named Andrew Rock. Andrew was two years my senior and ran similar events (200m and 400m). His dad, Alan, helped out at practice, and I thought to myself, *These guys seem to know what they're doing.* I'd run with that group, always a few seconds behind Andrew, but close enough that I felt I belonged. While Andrew Rock would go on to compete in track at the University of Wisconsin La Crosse, a Division 3 school in southwestern Wisconsin, I don't think anyone realized that he still wasn't close to acheiving his full potential. After working his way up in the professional ranks, Rock began to run for Team USA. In 2004, Rock would win an Olympic gold medal in the 4x400 relay in Athens, Greece.

The 400-meter dash was my event, and my development was obviously aided by guys like Adam, Garry II, and Andrew training next to me. As simple as this sounds, having people around you that are better than you is the best way to improve. Running in the 9-10-year-old category, I finished fourth at the state meet as a nine-year-old. I knew the following year would be my opportunity, and after setting a regional record at the qualifying meet, I had two weeks to prepare for the state meet at the end of June. It was the only time in my life that I actually felt a bit pushed from my father. He told me simply that it was up to me what I did the next two weeks and that he didn't want me to regret not giving it my best shot. Heeding his advice, I'd go out in front on my house and run the length of my street, which was about 400 meters. Winning aside, I just wanted to run fast.

We woke up at about 4:00 a.m. on a Saturday morning and made the two and half hour drive to Madison, WI. About half way there, my dad got pulled over and then got ticketed because I was sleeping, reclined in the back seat, and wasn't wearing a seat belt. Half asleep, I felt bad, as my dad explained to the officer that we were on our way to the Badger State Games track meet, but it didn't seem to matter.

Distractions aside, there is nothing more nerve wracking than approaching the starting line in a track race and waiting for that gun to go off. My competitors came strolling out with fancy warm-ups, spandex running suits, and spiked shoes. My gray, cotton shorts and Nike Air Pegasus made me feel a bit out of place, but I thought to myself, *Don't worry about any of that.* Thinking back to the sprints in front of my house, I knew I was prepared and told myself, *Run your race.* Never a fan of starting blocks for the 400, I was the only runner to start in an upright position, leaning forward slightly with my head down.

Bang! Running in a white "MYTC" tank top, I got off to a slight lead before evening out with my competitors after the first 100 meters. I liked the 400 because you had to run as hard as you could, but it was a long way for a ten-year-old, meaning that the last 100 meters was all heart. Coming around the final bend, I could feel my heart pounding and was acutely aware of the sounds of my breaths. My mind was blank, and in the moment, I could feel my body tiring. I was hurting. All of the sprints in front of my house, though, were done to be able to finish this last 100 meters. I started my kick and pulled ahead slightly. With about 50 meters to go and the crowd cheering loudly from the grandstands, I heard a woman yell, "You're going to catch him!" Knowing that someone was right on my heels, a burst of adrenaline shot through my body, and it was exactly what I needed to hang on. I crossed the finish line and collapsed to my knees, knowing that I was a state champion. I received a gold medal and stood atop the podium, with Dr. Martin and the rest of the MYTC family smiling proudly. Nick Polk, a nine-year-old from Milwaukee, finished third in that race. Nick would go on to start at free safety for Indiana University and later play in the NFL. To say competition starts early is an understatement.

In the early 1990's, Marshfield Columbus High School had a great athletic tradition in the Wisconsin Independent School Athletic Association or WISAA, which was made up of all of the private schools in the state of Wisconsin. Prep fans will recall the great Walt Kroll, who ran a powerhouse football program at

Columbus and churned out state titles year after year (seven total to be exact). I would attend Columbus sporting events with my dad and nestle into the packed venues for both football and basketball games. As a young boy, the games were tremendously motivating to me. I wanted to be out on that field and court someday, and I couldn't imagine how great it must have been to play in front of so many people. I'll never forget Justin Casperson hitting a guy so hard that he lost his helmet and was taken off the field in a stretcher. Years later, Mike Scheuer would star at quarterback, and my mom, an occupational therapist, brought me home an autographed note from Scheuer after he was hospitalized from a car accident (probably not the best time to ask for an autograph!). Scheuer would recover and later become an All-American defensive back at the University of Wisconsin La Crosse.

The following summer, I went back to Columbus basketball camp, and Coach Orr seemed to take interest in me as a player. "Come on Johnny!" he'd yell as loud as he could, spit flying from his mouth. At the end of each camp session, we were separated into teams and got to play 5 on 5. In third grade, most kids are still running around, with no clue about what's going on. As I brought the ball up the floor, on each possession, Orr would yell out a different offensive move that he wanted me to try. "Cross it over, between the legs, behind the back, stutter step!" he'd yell with excitement. After the games were over, I told Orr how hard it was to dribble the ball between the legs while moving at full speed. Almost as if he had just won a new car, his face lit up and he smiled. "All of the kids here will go home and won't touch a basketball until the season starts in the fall. I want you to work on the things we did this week when you go home." So, that's what I did. I showed my brothers and sister the drills and would go out on my driveway and practice. As I improved, it became hard not to incorporate some kind of ball handling routine into my day. Again, I was never pushed, but I trusted Mr. Orr, and quite honestly, I didn't know any better.

Because of the brutal cold winters in central Wisconsin, my family spent a lot of time at our local YMCA. The "Y" had two pools, two basketball courts, weights, and fitness equipment, and my whole family would go to get some form of exercise. I spent a lot of time in the gym, watching older guys and waiting my turn to get picked for 5 on 5 games. There was one guy in particular who really stood out. His name was Noel Dartt, and he was a sophomore at Marshfield Senior High School. Noel was a long, rangy athlete, about 6'3", and seemed to be at the "Y" every time I was there. Not only was Noel a good player, but I think he appreciated the fact that I'd do the drills I was taught on a side hoop while I waited and would pick me to play on his team when guys would go up and down. Being the oldest child, it was fun to have an "older brother" of sorts. As much as I didn't want to let Noel down when we played, it gave me confidence when older kids were available for him to pick, and yet he'd say, "I want John." Equally important, I'd watch intently how Noel handled the ball, got to the basket in limited dribbles, and created space to shoot. Seeing these things done day after day made it easier for me to visualize myself doing the same things. I'd look to Noel for feedback, and he'd often tell me to keep my head up when I led the fast break. "Dribble less and pass the ball up the floor." On defense, the message was simple, "Keep your guy in front of you," he'd say.

_Keep it simple_

On July 21, 1995, Noel Dartt was killed in a car accident about a mile from my house. My parents had heard about the accident and told me the news. At the time, I was too young to know how to react. It was hard for me to explain to anyone that I had spent quite a bit of time with Noel Dartt, and my immaturity didn't prompt me to speak up about attending the wake or the funeral.

I spent the rest of that summer thinking that death was a real thing that apparently could take any of us at a given moment. Shooting on a side hoop at the YMCA, I'd ask the older guys if I could play but get laughed at because of my age. My "big brother" and the only basketball mentor I had known, aside from my father and Coach Orr, was dead. I wish I had been able to describe how hurt I was. Instead, I told myself that crying about it wasn't going to get me anywhere. I needed to get tougher and be able to hold my own, both as a basketball player and as a person. I worked hard on my game the next few months and took things a bit more seriously, all while starting the fifth grade.

Because of the extreme winter climate in central Wisconsin, I didn't have anywhere else to play outside of our trips to the YMCA and basketball practice twice a week at St. John's school. Our basement at the Willkom house was partially finished, and the back was open cement that housed our water heater and foundational poles that held our house up. It was cold and damp down there and dimly lit, with yellowish light bulbs and random bins of things in storage. Every night, I'd go down there, turn on the radio, and work on my ball handling. What started as just stationary drills with one and two basketballs, turned into chair drills and other change of direction work. I'd set up old folding chairs and move whatever I could out of the way to create as much space as possible. That water heater must've gotten crossed-over more than ten thousand times! Following each workout, I'd work on my jumping, attempting to touch the ceiling as many times as I could before I couldn't. I'd do sit ups, push-ups, and calf raises on our steps. Occasionally, one of my siblings would join me, but more out of me "selling" them on the benefits than their true desire to participate. There were a lot of days when I didn't feel like going down those twelve stairs. And it was lonely. But, I started to fall in love with the process of improvement. I'd show up on Saturday mornings to play our weekly city league game and play better each week.

In sixth grade, I had the opportunity to be a water boy for the Marshfield Columbus football team, along with Luke Knauf and Sam Klumb, who attended St. John's with me. It was a special season, led by a special group of athletes. Mike Weister was a star at running back and would go on to play at South Dakota. Jason Linzmeier played wide receiver but was better known for his talent on the basketball court, where he would eventually play at Winona State University. The spirit that carried that team, though, came from Rich Seubert, who would go on to play at Western Illinois as an offensive lineman and later for ten seasons as a guard for the New York Giants. Rich was as tough as they come. He'd play both ways and just maul people. At 6'5", 240 pounds, he wasn't as big as he'd become, but he had a JJ Watt-type of attitude. Columbus won the Division 3 state title that year, 42-6, led by Weister's 208 yards rushing. As a young boy, it was special to stand on the field at Camp Randall stadium (home of the Wisconsin Badgers) and watch those guys hoist a gold ball into the air. More importantly, it set a tone for me about how championship players compete. Those guys put in the time, both working on their skills and developing their bodies, and it showed on the field. And unlike most fans, I had witnessed a lot of the behind-the-scenes work, which often left me thinking, *How can these guys not win?* To grow up in a small town and get the opportunity to be around guys like that was an opportunity I was always grateful for.

Later that year, I was playing in a basketball tournament in Spencer, WI, and the game was tied with less than a minute to play. Battling underneath, I grabbed a rebound and laid the ball up, while Spencer's Frank Searer hacked my right hand. And one! Immediately, I knew something was wrong, and I ran over to my coach, as my right pinkie finger was hanging off to the side and clearly broken. We'd win that game and the tournament, but I had to be fitted for a splint and was told my season was over.

I was devastated. Our city league tournament was a week away, and we had a title to defend. It was early March, and their was still quite a bit of snow on the ground in central Wisconsin. Broken finger or not, every day after school that week, I'd bundle up and shoot left-handed free throws on my driveway until it would get dark. In two years of playing organized basketball, I had never lost a game, and a small injury wasn't going to derail that. Later that week, after multiple conversations with my parents, they agreed to let me play in a splint that a hand therapist that worked with my mom molded for me.

I knew I still had the quickness to get by people, but I would be limited to only driving to my left. Regardless, we were playing for a city championship, and I was going to be out on that floor. In one of the most unsportsmanlike strategies I had ever seen, the other team's coach was instructing his kids to "hack" me. On my first catch of the ball at the top of the key, he yelled, "Foul him" and demonstrated with his arms what he wanted done. It was one thing to foul someone; it was another to blatantly hack my right hand, which was all wrapped up. Sending me to the line multiple times, I hit 6-8 free throws, left-handed, and we won the game.

# 3

# JOE'S ALL STARS

In seventh grade, students from Our Lady of Peace (OLP) and St. John's elementary schools combined to attend Holy Family Middle School (HFMS), which was a part of Marshfield Columbus High School. In two years, I had never lost a game to another team in Marshfield. OLP always finished second, and I knew those kids would either be happy to team with me or bitter about the past two seasons. Following a regular season, we took our talents on the road in February, March, and April and went to head-to-head with the best teams in the state of Wisconsin. Wearing jerseys that said, "HFMS" on the front, we didn't lose a game that entire spring. After putting together dominant performances to beat the Sun Prairie Hoops Club, La Crosse McDonald's All Stars, and Eau Claire Gators, people began to question the makeup of our team. At every tournament, we would get asked the same questions: "What schools do you guys go to? What radio station sponsors you? How did you recruit each other to join forces?" When all of us replied that we attended the same school and explained that HFMS was an acronym for a middle school in Marshfield and not a radio station, it still seemed to elicit confused looks from the questioners. The reason was probably because we were beating elite, all-star teams from all over the state. Our competition often had kids from more than ten cities on one team, and these teams were pulling from major metro areas. As complicated as everyone else thought it was, we all went to a small, Catholic school together and grew up in the same community. How did we win six straight tournaments?

The answer started with our coach, Joe Konieczny. Joe was a former state champion at Marshfield Columbus and set several three-point shooting records during his time there. I knew Joe could shoot, but I had no idea how this guy would change my life in a mere three months. Practicing two or three times per week, Joe ran collegiate level practices for seventh-graders. The first time I met Joe, he looked at my black shoes and socks and said bluntly, "You need to wear white socks." We pressed 100% of the time and worked on ball handling drills every single practice. We'd partner up and go as hard as we could for thirty seconds and then rotate. "Next guy up! Ready! Go!" Joe would yell. As drills would wind down, Joe always seemed to be in my ear: "Ten more seconds, Johnny! Just ten more seconds!"

Our goal was simple: turn our opponents over and push the basketball. We also did a large amount of conditioning. Joe was famous for the "ten wall", which was a series of sprints ten lengths of the floor in under a minute. Although I wasn't used to that level of conditioning, my attitude throughout my entire career was always the same: you have to be in tremendous shape to play at the highest level. I'll never forget panting and struggling out to the old water fountain in the foyer of Our Lady of Peace gymnasium where we practiced. There were multiple times when I'd stand there, bent over at the waist, and think about quitting. I didn't "have" to do this. Then, I'd glance over at my teammates, who looked just as bad as I did. None of us were used to being pushed to that level. That first month was brutal, like "I'm gonna die brutal." Despite subzero temperatures in February, we'd often step outside during breaks just to cool down. I probably lost between ten and fifteen pounds during my three months with Joe, and for the first time in my life, started to really look like an athlete. More importantly, though, I developed an attitude that hard work translates into winning. Put

*conditioning this year twice as hard as my opponents*

simply, I was tougher. In tight games or moments of fatigue, I'd think about those nights, in that old, dark gym. No one was there to see it, other than the guys on my team, and I took solace in believing that I had worked twice as hard as my opponent. It's hard to make the statement that you deserve to win but playing for Joe made me feel that way.

*AFTER mistake*

Joe also had a special way of getting the best out of me. He had identified a personality characteristic that channeled all of his feedback to me in a positive manner. Instead of getting on my case for a bad pass or turnover, Joe would look me in the eye, smile, and say, "You're better than that. Don't make the same mistake twice."

*what went you thinking?*

Later in the year, we were losing to a team that was much taller and physically developed. At halftime, we all felt a bit beaten down, and Joe walked into the locker room and simply said, "If I could handpick a team, I wouldn't trade a single guy on our squad. Every single one of you is more skilled than those guys. Every single one of you has worked harder the past three months. When those guys were sitting at home, you were getting better." Winning starts with a belief, and that belief starts with a leader.

*that*

In mid-March, Joe had t-shirts printed for all of us that simply said, "Joe's All Stars" on the front, with our last name and number on the back. It was a subtle joke to those who doubted the make-up of our team, but also a strong affirmation that we belonged at the biggest and best tournaments. I wore mine with pride and spent most of my summer between seventh and eighth grade meeting Joe at the Marshfield YMCA for individual workouts.

For the first time in my life, I had found a person outside of my family that held me to a higher standard. While Noel Dartt had been an on-court mentor to me, Joe was a life mentor. Average wasn't good enough for Joe and that pertained to more than just basketball. He became my confirmation sponsor and actively encouraged me to pursue a relationship with God. When it came to alcohol and drugs, he flat out looked at me one day and said, "If I ever hear that you're doing that, I will come over and beat the shit

*told them to a higher standard*

out of you."

Joe's All Stars was a special time in my life, not because we won a bunch of games, but because I was surrounded by other guys that loved the game of basketball. The tough practices and brutal conditioning sessions were all masked by the fact that I could look every single guy on that team in the eye, and I had 100% trust that they wanted what I wanted.

It was also the first time I felt completely secure with myself. We often go through life either feeling like we don't have the skills or the confidence to be who we want to be. I knew I had to continue to get better, but I'd also tell myself, *You're good enough*, which I believe gave me the confidence to fully express my skills on the basketball court.

As Joe's All Stars came to an end, so did our apparent state championship team in the making at Marshfield Columbus. Living a few blocks from Marshfield Senior High School, I decided to transfer to the public school after my freshman year. There, I would have better academic opportunities and access to more AP classes. Despite making rational sense, it was one of the toughest decisions I've ever had to make. In hindsight, you realize how rare it was to share a vision of excellence with a team. There was a military-like bond, trust, and collective willingness to do whatever it took. I'd argue that most people never fully experience that in their lifetime.

A year later, Luke Knauf and Mike Wilke, both key cogs on our team, transferred to Stratford High School, and Eric Kraus, another starting forward, joined me at Marshfield Senior High. Luke would go on to a decorated football career at Stratford, where he was named the state's offensive player of the year by the Wisconsin Football Coaches Association as a senior. To win that award as a 6'5", 290 lb. lineman tells you all you need to know about Luke. Would Luke Knauf have achieved at that level without the influence of Rich Seubert six years earlier? Similar to the influence of Noel Dartt, Kevin Orr, and Joe Konieczny on me, I think one of life's greatest blessings is to have people in your life that you can pattern. We all owe it to future generations to provide an example of a life worth emulating. It's worth mentioning that the defensive player of the year award went to Joe Thomas, who would go on to be one of the best left tackles ever to play in the NFL.

Even after the multiple transfers, Marshfield Columbus made a trip to Madison for the State Tournament during our senior year of high school, losing to Greg Steimsma and eventual state champion, Randolph (Steimsma would go on to play for the Wisconsin Badgers and for several NBA teams). To this day, I still think about what could have been and the style of game that we would have brought to the state tournament. Four guards that could score and one forward/center. The makeup wasn't as special as the chemistry, as we had a knack for making each other better and maximizing each other's talents. My coach at Marshfield Senior High told me that he had never seen a team pass the ball like we did in seventh and eighth grade.

# 4

# CAMPS & AAU

I began to play Amateur Athletic Union (AAU) basketball as it started to become popular in Wisconsin. AAU is simply a tournament system for teams to play in the spring and summer. People close to the game view AAU as the best means to get noticed by college coaches. Following my freshman year of high school, Luke Knauf and I had the opportunity to play on the original Reebok sponsored Fox Valley Skillz. Richie Davis started the program, and we had a deep and talented roster, full of mostly guys from the Fox Valley area in eastern Wisconsin. Notable players included Brian Butch (Appleton West), Steve Hoelzel (Kaukauna), Tyrone Deacon (Bay Port), Josh Schneider (St. Mary's Springs), and Chris Kellett (Neenah). Playing for the Skillz was an awesome opportunity to play against great players and travel the country. During the spring and summer of 2000, we played in tournaments in Madison and Milwaukee (WI), Kearney (NE), Fort Wayne (IN), Akron (OH), and Las Vegas (NV).

The Spiece Run & Slam Classic in Fort Wayne was particularly memorable to me because we made a deep tournament run before losing in the final four to former Xavier & Oklahoma point guard Andrew Lavender and All Ohio Red. Before we played the guys from Ohio, we took on Shannon Brown and the Illinois Warriors. The Warriors were loaded with talent and speed, while we had a considerable size advantage with 6'11" Brian Butch in the middle. Between Tyrone, Dean Furton (Marinette), and I, we managed to keep Brown (Michigan State & NBA) and point guard, Charles Richardson (Nebraska), in check and won a tight game. While I remember winning the game, I'll never forget the breakaway dunk by Shannon Brown, in which he literally jumped over Tyrone, who was attempting to take a charge in the middle of the lane. Brown dunked, yelled out in excitement, and went to the free throw line. At the time, I thought, *Whatever man, you're still losing*. And he did lose, but man, that dunk was nasty!

Following another game in that same tournament, the opposing team was huddled up at center court. As I sat on our bench and changed my shoes, I watched the coaching staff hand guys cash. I thought to myself that it must be for lunch money. But, with the way travel basketball has evolved over the years, that money probably wasn't for hot dogs.

Playing in Akron, Ohio, was special because the tournament was held at St. Vincent St. Mary's High School, where a kid named LeBron James had just finished his freshman year. While LeBron wasn't there, we lost to his high school teammates in the championship game. Several of those kids would go on to play college sports, including Dru Joyce III, Sian Cotton, Willie McGee, and Romeo Travis. They also went on to win three state championships and were inducted into the school's athletic Hall of Fame in August 2011. Let me remind you that this was the summer between my freshman and sophomore years of high school. Between games, I was sitting in the school's cafeteria eating a sandwich, and I noticed a cardboard cut-out set up in the corner of the room of LeBron. Seriously, how many fifteen-year-olds have a cardboard cutout in their high school cafeteria?! Lebron was taking the city of Akron by storm, and the rest of the country would soon follow.

Most of us rode out to Ohio in a motor home driven by Josh Schneider's dad. We had so much fun on that bus, which included being "mooned" by an entire baseball team as their bus passed us on the freeway.

Our last tournament of the summer was in Las Vegas for the Adidas Big Time. Imagine a group of fifteen-year-old Wisconsin guys walking on the Vegas Strip. After one of our games, we went to the Nascar Café to ride a roller coaster and were approached by three extremely large men. "Excuse us guys," they said. They explained to us that Britney Spears and her sister were going to ride the coaster and would appreciate it if we let them go to the front of the line. Britney or not, I had been waiting for an hour to ride this thing! But my emotions settled, and more importantly, the size of the three men became incredibly clear to me. "Go right ahead," we all said in one form or another. Britney came strolling through, and it almost looked like she was walking in slow motion. I smiled at her, and she smiled back, waved, and in a cheery voice exclaimed, "Thanks guys!" At a time with no social media or cell phones (none of our parents would allow us to have one), we had to tell all our friends how amazing she looked in person!

As far as the basketball, we played well in Vegas, and it was fun (and nerve-racking) to play in front of Roy Williams, Mike Krzyzewski, Tom Crean, Bo Ryan, and several other big-time college coaches. Of course, they were all there to see 6'11" Brian Butch (who would later commit to Wisconsin), but who knew? With all of those coaches in attendance for our first game, I picked a kid's pocket and sprinted down the right side of the floor. In a surreal moment, I lobbed the ball up to Neenah High School's Chris Kellet, who threw down the alley-oop. Any questions around whether we belonged were answered, and I left Vegas knowing that I could hold my own against the best kids in the United States. The year 2000 also marked the appearance of a kid named LeBron James at Adidas Big Time. At the time, George Karl, who was then head coach of the Milwaukee Bucks, was quoted as saying people should come and watch this kid before they have to pay hundreds of dollars for seats in four years. Man, was he right.

I played AAU basketball the next two summers with Valley Bay, another Fox Valley area team, which was coached by Russ Hansen. Russ's son, Nick, played on the team and would go on to play at UW-Milwaukee. All in all, most of my AAU teammates went on to play college sports: Brian Butch (Wisconsin), Steve Hoelzel (UW-Milwaukee/UW-Eau Claire), Tyrone Deacon (Michigan State/UW-Parkside), Kenny DeBauche (Wisconsin Football), Luke Knauf (Wisconsin Football), Dean Furton (UW-Eau Claire), Chris Kellett (Ripon College), and Josh Schneider (Winona State).

In addition to AAU, I attended a lot of camps. Some were focused on providing exposure to college coaches, while others were all about skill development. Camps like Van Coleman's Future Stars in Iowa, The Wisconsin Basketball Yearbook's Exposure Camp, or the University of Wisconsin's Elite Camp provided a great stage to play in front of a lot of college coaches. Because AAU was still on the upswing, these camps had more value than they do now because players could truly be "discovered."

As an eighth-grader, I went head to head with Jeff Horner, who was a ninth- grader from Mason City, IA. Jeff was physically mature at a young age, could easily dunk the ball at 6'2", and was already verbally committed to Iowa. Mike Henderson was my age and another Iowa commit. At the time, Mike was so much better than the rest of us because of his physical maturity. He would go on to have a solid career at Iowa, but he didn't grow another inch after eighth grade! At Future Stars, I competed against another Iowa kid who was about 6'6" and had deep range. He'd go on to star at Creighton, and the rest of the world would eventually figure out that Kyle Korver could really shoot the ball.

The exposure camps provided top notch competition and the college coaches to boot. If you ever needed a measuring stick as to what Division 1 recruits looked like, these events were it. I'd leave those camps motivated to work harder. As much as the Marshfield community had provided a basketball foundation, I needed to leave Marshfield to understand that their was another level out there.

Before I could ever attend an exposure camp, though, I needed to start with skill development camps. The first overnight basketball camp I ever attended was at UW-Stevens Point (UWSP) led by Jack Bennett. Jack's brother, Dick, coached at the University of Wisconsin, and Dick's son, Tony, has done a phenomenal job as the head coach at the University of Virginia. My brother and I would go for three or four days, and we always had a great time. At an early age, Ken Koelbl, one of UWSP's assistant coaches, came up to me one day at camp and said, "I really like the way you play. I'm going to have Coach Bennett come watch one of your next camp games."

The next day at camp, sure enough, Coach Bennett was there for the whole game. Afterwards, he came up to me and said, "I really like the way you pass the ball." I'll never forget that. We chatted for a bit, and he told me he'd be keeping an eye on me. I was eleven years old. _Willingness to work!_

Bennett gave a departing speech to all of the campers the following evening, and he said, "You have to possess two traits to be successful. You have to be willing, and you have to be able. He provided some color around what that meant, but the bottom line is that a guy without a work ethic is worthless, even if he has all the ability in the world, and vice versa. He challenged every camper to identify the weaknesses in our game and then bring the right attitude to the improvement process. I loved that speech.

The best camp I ever attended, though, was the Prairie du Chien Perimeter Camp in southwestern Wisconsin. The camp was for grades seven to twelve, and the two and half day camp had three, three-hour sessions per day. After a couple years, the camp had gotten so popular that kids would be bussed around to several gyms in the area. Due to limited space, we'd often do ball handling drills in school cafeterias or hallways. The gyms were hot, and most weren't air conditioned. Lodging also became a challenge, and my best friend, Luke Knauf, and I walked into an old motel room one year that had one king-sized bed with a huge mirror over the top!

At night, buses would take anyone that wanted to go to a large, indoor pool, that was actually located on prison grounds. The pool area was dark but had lights under the water that created an eerie effect. Large windows loomed above the water on a second level, where coaches were hanging out to "supervise."

If you were serious about the game, this was arguably one of the best camps in the entire country. Led by legendary high school coach, Forrest Larson, the camp was incredibly high energy and was set up to challenge the best of the best. Forrest had run camps for coaches like Tom Davis at Iowa, Billy Donovan at Florida, and Dick Bennett at Wisconsin. Former Marshfield Columbus coach, Andy Banasik, was the head coach at Prairie du Chien High School and set the camp up. In addition to Banasik, my former elementary school gym teacher, Kevin Orr, was on the staff, as was Colby (WI) High School head coach, Dave Macarthur. The camp was all perimeter based, but if you thought it would be a 50/50 split between ball handling and shooting, you were dead wrong. Jeff Boos, the coach at Sun Prairie High School (WI), got about 5% of the time to teach shooting. The other 95% was full speed footwork, ball handling, and learning to create space. Music blared from the speakers, whistles blew constantly, and every thirty seconds to a minute, you were expected to give all-out effort. In two and half days, I probably dribbled around more than a thousand cones and chairs, while listening to every Jock Jams song every produced.

It was great to re-connect with Coach Orr, who was coaching at Elgin Academy (IL) and was contemplating a move back to Wisconsin to be closer to family. I'll save you several years, but Coach Orr did move back to Wisconsin and took a high school girls' job in a small town called Rice Lake to do so. "Family first," as he used to say, but we all knew he missed coaching boys.

Coach Orr would eventually become the boys coach at Rice Lake high school, and in an act straight from the basketball gods, two kids named Wally and Henry Ellenson transferred to play for him. Both brothers would go on to play for Marquette, with Henry getting drafted by the Detroit Pistons in the 2016 NBA Draft.

While several of us cheered as we watched on television, a cameo of a stoic Orr applauding the pick flashed on the screen. His hair was now a salty gray and his energy a bit scaled back from when I had first met him, but his passion for the game of basketball had never wavered. It was a moment of sheer joy and deep reflection for me, as Orr had always put himself second, and there he was, sitting in the Barclays Center, in Brooklyn, NY, the proud coach of an NBA first-round draft pick.

Forrest Larson was the perfect example of someone I feared, yet respected. His son, Brent, was a ball-handling wizard and would go on to have a successful college career at the University of Wisconsin Stevens Point. This was all before YouTube was popular, so getting to see a guy like Brent in person was exciting. When Forrest would get angry, he never swore but would loudly exclaim, "God bless America!"

Forrest did a lot of demonstrations, and it was a big deal when Forrest pulled you out of the crowd to demonstrate a drill. My first year at camp, Brent would demonstrate everything. Brent walked around like his ankles were permanently sprained; I couldn't tell if that was from thousands of hours of ball handling drills, or if he just had bad ankles. Brent was unbelievably skilled with the basketball and even better during two ball drills. Forrest told us that when Brent was a little kid, he'd bribe him with things like an ice cream cone if he could do more than fifty switch-ems (crossing two basketballs in front of your body) in a minute. As much as all of us thought we performed at a similar skill level, it wasn't close. Over the next few years, Forrest would pull me out of the seated crowd of hundreds of campers to demonstrate several times. The first time he called my name, my heart just started pounding. *What if I screwed up?* But the more I got to know Forrest, the more I realized he actually wanted me to make mistakes. "Full speed Willkom!" he'd shout. Mistakes meant you were challenging yourself, and as demanding as Forrest was, there wasn't a day where I'd leave the gym thinking, *I didn't get any better today.*

During my senior year of high school in 2003, Forrest would lead Ladysmith High School to a Wisconsin state championship, handing Auburndale their only loss of the season. Auburndale was located ten minutes outside of my hometown of Marshfield, and I had grown up playing against those guys. As much I would've liked to see them win a gold ball, I watched a less-talented Ladysmith team execute on all cylinders, and I couldn't help but admire what I was watching.

Later, Larson would go on to coach at Lake Geneva Badger High School in southeastern Wisconsin. When interviewed by the Milwaukee Journal Sentinel regarding the job, Forrest said, "We want to be the hardest working team in the state of Wisconsin. I don't know why we can't be that. Someone has to be the hardest working team and in the future, I hope it's going to be Badger High School." (Roquemore)

Unlike other camps, where I'd come home and encourage my buddies to go the next year, most of my friends never went to the Prairie du Chien Perimeter Camp. It wasn't that they couldn't afford it or didn't have the time, but they knew that if I thought it was hard, then it must be pretty damn hard. And it made sense. I mean, who, when given the choice, would put themselves through two and a half days of hell?

Going to Prairie taught me a valuable lesson about life, and that is so many things seem intimidating before you begin. Every rationale thought reminds you why you shouldn't participate. And yet, if you do muscle up the courage to attend and put everything you possibly have into it and then a bit more when you have nothing left, you come out a warrior on the other side. The beauty is that every time you can't breathe and you mentally want to quit, that one extra set of drills or that additional thirty seconds is what sets you apart from everyone else the rest of your life.

Going back to my friends, the child in me wanted them to be there, but the competitor in me knew I was getting better, while they were sitting around at home. I owe a great deal to Coach

Larson, Coach MacArthur, Coach Orr, Coach Boos, and Coach Banasik for not only motivating me but teaching me what it meant to "work."

Between my experiences at Prairie's camp and playing for Joe Konieczny, I started to develop an actual love for the game. As I laid in bed one night, I thought, *These guys could be doing anything, and they choose to spend nine hours a day in a gym with no air conditioning! Why do they do it? Why do they care so much?*

Being around great players and going to camps like Prairie, I was motivated to try something following my senior year of high school. I wanted to start my own basketball camp. My friend, Mike Lee, a former state champion at Marshfield Columbus High School and guard at the University of Wisconsin Stout, had attended a lot of the same camps I had, as well as team camps at several high-major universities. We both agreed that a perimeter-focused skill development camp was missing in central Wisconsin, and so we did what any reasonable folks would do: we started our own. The Marshfield Perimeter Camp was launched in 2003, and we hired Colby's Dave Macarthur to lead our camp.

Dave was built like a brick and stood about 6'2", with broad shoulders and a balding hairline. When Dave was around, it was impossible not to know. He was loud, enthusiastic, energetic, and intense. His demeanor and personality reminded me a lot of NFL coach, Jon Gruden, and having worked the Prairie du Chien camps, he understood what we were trying to build. Dave had grown up in Ladysmith, WI, which is where he had met Forrest Larson as a senior in high school. Following graduation, Dave played for two seasons at the University of Wisconsin Marshfield/Wood County (The Wood), where he was named the Wisconsin Junior College Conference Player of the Year in 1991. He would transfer to the University of Wisconsin La Crosse and later serve as an assistant student coach there for two years before returning to The Wood as the head coach. The thing about Dave that separated him from so many other coaches was that he truly loved kids, and he loved basketball. It all sounds cliché, but there wasn't a day when you looked at Dave and didn't think to yourself, *This guy was born to do this.* On the very first day of camp, Dave overheard some kids debating whether to play basketball or join the wrestling team. "Would you rather grab another guy's balls or put the ball in the hole!" he exclaimed.

We had so much fun and argued every day during our lunch break, where we'd sit in a room eating Subway sandwiches and talk about players, teams, drills, and everything else basketball. There was a passion there that you can't make up and being around a guy like that just made you love the game. Dave had coached Mike Lee's AAU team a few years earlier, and he told guys at the first practice to call him anytime if they wanted to work out. A couple guys decided to mess with him and called him one night at one o'clock in the morning. Dave promptly answered the phone and simply said, "Meet me at the gym in fifteen minutes." He then proceeded to put them through a workout that I'm sure they've never forgotten.

That first year, we had almost a hundred kids attend camp at the Marshfield YMCA. We had music blaring, other area basketball standouts as coaches, and "Drill 4 Skill" t-shirts for every camper. Parents loved that their kids came home exhausted, and we got a lot of complements for bringing something "new" to the area.

The following summer, our attendance almost doubled, and we added a disc jockey to make the camp more exciting. Under Dave's leadership, parents were driving their kids up to three hours one way to attend. Joe Konieczny had become the head coach at Marshfield Columbus High School and graciously allowed us to host the camp there to have a larger gym space. Our t-shirt slogan read: "Anything you can do, you can do better," and it served us as coaches as much at it served the campers.

In year three, the popularity of the camp exploded, and we started a basketball camp circuit in the Midwest, where we held thirteen camps in thirteen different cities. Since the camp wasn't just in

Marshfield anymore, we re-branded to "Playmakers Basketball Camp." In the summer of 2005, we led more than two thousand campers and took the brand to another level by launching a digital store, video series, and The Blueprint, which was a training guide to help players maximize off season workouts. In addition, we started our own AAU program called the Wisconsin Playmakers, which would give kids in central and northern Wisconsin an opportunity that we didn't have locally growing up. The Playmakers still run a great program led by Jason Jesperson, and alumni Paul Jesperson (Virginia/Northern Iowa), Connor Miller (Samford/Minnesota State), and Matt Thomas (Iowa State) put us on the map at several big tournaments. The Wisconsin Playmakers now field both boys' and girls' teams for grades six to twelve.

Before our fourth summer, Dave received his master's degree in general education from the University of Wisconsin Stevens Point and was quietly building a big-time program at Colby High School, having won conference titles the past two seasons. Following the 2005-2006 campaign, Dave was selected as an assistant coach for the prestigious Wisconsin Basketball Coaches Association (WBCA) All Star Game, and we were all proud to see him get recognized. Dave and Joe had become close friends, as both employed a similar style of pressing, guard-oriented basketball that made watching the games a real treat for those in attendance.

In the fall of 2006, tragedy struck. Dave MacArthur had been out deer hunting, and when he didn't return for lunch, his wife walked out to check on him. Sitting in a tree stand, motionless, Dave had taken a drink of Coca-Cola and aspirated (essentially the Coca-Cola had entered his lungs). "He was drinking a bottle of Coke and the best (the pathologist) could describe is that David aspirated some of the Coca-Cola and since he was hunting, he was trying to suppress the cough," his wife said. "His coughing induced the vomiting, and then he passed out" (Associated Press). There were so many questions and so few answers. The energy, the passion, the love for people, all somehow gone in an instant at the age of 36.

I went to bed for weeks thinking about Dave and replaying that scenario in my mind. Sitting in the Colby High School gymnasium a few days later, Forrest Larson, his mentor and friend, delivered a powerful eulogy about a coach, teacher, husband, and father that left even the most stoic men in tears.

To this day, I still think about Dave MacArthur and pray for him every night before I go to sleep. He was one of the greatest men I ever knew. I don't say that to patronize him; I say it because I never spent a bad day with him. His mental fortitude was unbelievable. If I even started to complain about something, he'd look at me and laugh like I was crazy. "Come on Johnny, get over it! Today is a great day!"

# 5

# CROOKSTON

I had a productive high school career at Marshfield Senior High School. Three time all-conference, three-time all-area, and a 13-game winning streak my senior year that ended in a sectional loss to conference rival Wausau East. Playing for coach Gordie Sisson was an honor because he truly cared about kids. Every year, he'd drive an SUV full of guys westward to watch UW-Green Bay play. Win or lose, we'd stop at Kroll's, and he'd treat us to butter burgers. Sisson stood about 6'7" and physically demanded your attention but was a deep thinker, whose background as an English teacher often spilled over to the basketball court. He had a keen eye for recognizing good basketball but also had a great sense of humor. In 1994, he told a sub .500 team that if they advanced to the state tournament, he'd get a basketball tattoed on his ass. That team made a miraculous run through the playoffs, and let's just say the tattoo has held up nicely over the years. What I remember most about Coach Sisson, though, has nothing to do with basketball.

My high school held a year-end athletics banquet for all sports. It was a great way to recognize the accomplishments of the players, coaches, and families that had been a part of these successful teams. Following my sophomore season, I was recognized for an award. Coach Sisson stood proudly in the front of the banquet hall, shook my hand, and said a few things to me, before we turned for a photo.

A few hours later, the banquet ended, and my parents thanked Coach Sisson, while I stood there and listened to them talk. As proud as all of them were, Coach Sisson said, "Johnny did a hell of a job for us, but he didn't look me in the eye when I was trying to talk to him up there. I wish he would've looked me in the eye." Basketball and awards aside, the only thing he cared about that night was how I handled myself. As much as coaches across America claim to be in it to "develop young men," Coach Sisson walked the talk.

During my senior year of high school, I had narrowed down my college choices to the University of Minnesota Crookston and St. Mary's University in Winona, Minnesota. St. Mary's was a small, private school, of roughly six thousand students, and coach Bob Biebel did a tremendous job recruiting me. He was sincere and honest with me and my family, and I could tell that he loved the game by his facial expressions when he talked about it. Biebel also had ties to Appleton, WI, where my mother grew up, and specifically to Xavier High School, where my uncle had played point guard and grandfather taught history. Recruiting is such a tricky process because you never know who's telling you the truth, but I felt very comfortable with Coach Biebel, and I respected him as a person. He played at St. Mary's himself and constantly talked about how close he was to turning the program around.

To make a long story short, I committed to Crookston and Coach Jeff Oseth in April of my senior year. Looking back, I think I thought it was "cool" to receive an athletic scholarship, even though the actual amount of money was very comparable to what I would get in academic support from other schools (To clarify, only Division 1 and 2 schools can offer athletic scholarships. Division 3 schools will put academic packages together but can't offer official athletic scholarships). Signing a scholarship meant that I could have a signing day at my high school and sit for interviews with our local newspaper and radio people. As a high school senior, this is all flattering, and I think it distracts athletes from considering all factors when making their college decisions. Several kids have tremendous Division 3 offers, but they know they won't get the notoriety that accompanies a signing day. Several high schools now recognize Division 3 commitments to avoid exactly that.

Speaking of athletic scholarships, everyone seems to think that obtaining one is the greatest thing that can happen to a young person. If an academic scholarship pays the same amount, does it truly have greater value? Society and communities need to place greater emphasis on recognizing those that get rewarded for their grades so that young kids learn what a privilege it is to receive academic money to go to college.

Rants aside, I would have the next four months to prepare for my first season of college basketball, but it didn't mean that basketball would be the only thing occupying my time. Joe Konieczny, my middle school basketball coach and head coach at Marshfield Columbus High School, hired me to help his family's landscaping business. Let me tell you: mowing ditches and cemeteries all day can really take a toll on your body. After work, I would go home to grab a quick bite to eat, clean up, and then go straight to the gym so I could complete my summer strength and conditioning requirements that the Crookston basketball staff had laid out for me. I have the utmost respect for the men and women that do manual labor because it might seem fun for a day, but the rigors of doing the same thing day in and day out for a lifetime are mentally and physically taxing. By the end of each day, I didn't want to do anything besides go to sleep. Working as hard as I did that summer made me realize how privileged I was. There are millions of people that wake up every day, work long hours in hot sun or physically demanding jobs, and then come home and take care of a family. They are the true definition of servant leadership. And yet, here I was, working a summer job and playing basketball, and I thought the world was going to end. I will say that by the end of the summer, though, I was in tremendous shape, with tan skin that mimicked a Florida-retiree.

Talking to my teammates after I arrived at school, I was shocked to find out that none of them had followed the summer strength and conditioning program. In fact, they laughed at me because I was the only guy in the program that had actually completed the twelve-week agenda. I thought back to the lonely nights in the gym, often at nine or ten p.m., when my rational brain would tell me I had to get up for work at 5:30 a.m. the next day. It was literally screaming, "Go to bed!" But I didn't go to bed. I completed every day of that twelve-week program and pushed myself as hard as I could. Occasionally, YMCA staff or senior citizens walking around the running track, which looked down over the gym floor, would provide words of encouragement. A week later, fall conditioning began, and I set the program record for the 1.5-mile testing run.

To say that Crookston was cold would be an understatement. Winter there was like living in Antarctica. In fact, there were notices posted around campus dorms that read, "Please do not remain idle for more than five minutes, otherwise your limbs will freeze." That's a sign that everyone loves to read when they wake up in the morning. Anyways, my basketball experience at Crookston started immediately when I arrived with fall conditioning. I don't care if you're at Sisters of the Poor college or Duke, conditioning is always tough. The entire point is to push guys to their limits. Programs don't do conditioning anymore to get guys into shape; they do it to take already well-conditioned athletes and get them into elite shape. If I could ever give advice to anyone entering preseason conditioning, it would be to arrive in shape. Conditioning will always be as hard as it needs to be to make the most conditioned guy hurt. If you're in poor condition to start with, you will probably be hurting quite a bit more than your buddy that worked out all summer. And when I say hurting, I'm being polite: you'll be the guy puking in a garbage can.

We did a lot of running on the track or on the football field, often battling high winds and the pungent smell of the sugar beet fields next to campus. Our weight-lifting program wasn't overly strenuous. We'd lift with a partner of similar strength, but it's not like we had a strength coach breathing down our necks on every lift.

Lifting at Crookston was about lifting as much as you could and then possibly squeezing out a rep or two more with your partner's help. I worked hard in conditioning because I wanted to develop myself as an athlete. I was also 155 pounds, and like every other freshman, I needed to bulk up to withstand the rigors of playing against bigger and stronger guys.

I hate the guys that are always asking if conditioning is going to be hard today, or if weights will only be forty-five minutes instead of an hour. To me, everything was hard because I made it hard. Anybody can run around a track four or five times in a row. Even when the coaches were timing, I knew I could coast a bit and still crack the minute or so time limit to finish the lap (must have been those 400-meter races as a kid). Despite that, however, I ran as hard as I could because that's the way I do everything. I'm not the guy who's trying to be an ass-hole and make the guys that are dogging it look bad. However, if those guys aren't going hard in the preseason, then why would they go hard in the regular or post seasons? And, if the whole point is to push each other to get better, competitors want to be surrounded by other competitors. Conditioning was always tough for me because I made it that way, which was a mentality born from Coach Orr and embraced during my time with Joe. I was a workout warrior of sorts; a guy that sought out hard work because I thrived on the feeling of getting better. There is nothing more fulfiling than being able to walk into your apartment or dorm room and just collapse on the couch knowing that you've done your very best. I had that feeling pretty much every day, which was great because I knew I was working for a purpose, and each session meant that I was one day closer to starting the season.

Years later, I would meet a guy named Brian Nephew sitting in the stands watching NBA Summer League in Las Vegas. Brian had a wife and kids, worked in investments, and loved basketball. He told me that he missed that "pain and push" of being an athlete, and I knew exactly what he meant. When he left Vegas, I don't think either one of us knew what he was going to do to fill that void.

Six months later, he went heli-skiing, and then he started ultra-running. Since, he's run more events than can I count, with varying distances from 50-100 miles just to feel that pain again. Wow.

As the season approached, I was so excited. It's a special time of the year when you see Dickie V on ESPN talking about diaper dandies and preseason teams to watch. Being at a smaller school, we didn't have a midnight madness like the traditional Division 1 powers, which was fine because I didn't need fans there to watch me practice. That's why we have the games. The day before our first official practice, I was playing pick-up with the guys, and something happened that is the ultimate depressant for any college freshman: I got injured. The injury occurred on a routine pull up jump shot, but I landed on a teammate's foot, and I knew right away that my ankle was in trouble. To my relief, x-rays were negative, and the trainer told me to give it a "couple weeks." *A couple weeks! Are you kidding me?!* Here I was as a freshman trying to gain the confidence of my teammates and coaches, and all I could do was sit on the sideline. It was especially disappointing because I was coming off a tremendous preseason, and physically, I felt like I was right where I wanted to be.

Four practices went by, and three days later, I was on the floor, taped, and ready to compete. Practice was very physical, but I enjoyed it. For some reason, people don't realize what a brutal sport basketball is. If you have an opportunity to watch a college practice, especially in the preseason, you would be amazed at the physical play. Fights would break out every day because of the constant pushing and shoving that goes on. Guys would come back to the locker room with scratches all over and torn jerseys. One day, I was attempting to make a simple entry pass to the wing, and it was almost laughable watching my shooting guard getting tackled as he tried to get open. Unless you are the best player on a team, coaches will let players fight because they want them to respect each other, and they want tough players, both physically and mentally. I got in my fair share of scuffles, but I always had good intentions, and guys were cool when things calmed down.

Our first game of the season was at Division 2 power St. Cloud State (MN). St. Cloud was a nice school, and I had considered going there out of high school strictly to pursue a degree. My girlfriend at the time was a freshman there, and I was excited to see her, as well as my family, who would also be in attendance. I got in at about the twelve-minute mark and got a nice steal off a deflection. Coming down on the two on one, I dished the ball to a teammate who lost it out of bounds before he could finish the lay-up. I thought to myself, *If we can't score on that, we're going to be in trouble.* A few plays later, I hit a pull up jumper from the top of the key to record my first collegiate points. It felt great to score at that level, and even though I knew I belonged, it still was rewarding to "knock one down." We ended up losing the game by about twenty, but we played hard, and heads were high on the road trip home.

A couple weeks later, we headed to Seattle to play in a Thanksgiving tournament at Central Washington University. The coaching staff had decided to fly in a day early to tour the Seattle Supersonics practice facility. Because the team had lost the night before, we wouldn't be allowed at practice, but we did get to hang with the guys in the weight room.

One guy that stood out, literally, was Calvin Booth. Standing 6'11", Booth had a wingspan for days, and I laughed a bit watching him struggle to bench press 135 lbs. What wasn't laughable was his music choice, as he had the new G-Unit album blaring from the speakers.

The one guy that wasn't there was Ray Allen because he was busy getting treatment in the training room. Ray was one of my favorite players in the league after beginning his career in Milwaukee, and he just made the game look so easy. He also worked extremely hard and was a model citizen off the court.

Talking to the Sonic's strength coach, he explained that guys needed to get ten strength & conditioning sessions in each month. For every workout they missed, they were fined $5,000 by the team.

He said some guys actually accepted a fine because they felt ten sessions weren't necessary. The opposite was Ray Allen. He was in there almost every day working on his strength, flexibility, and stamina. Any betting man could've guessed his career was going to last a bit.

Following the weight room, we got a tour of the Sonics locker room, and Ray's locker was loaded with custom Jordan's.

That night, a bunch of the guys left the hotel after curfew for a night on the town. It set the wrong tone early in the season, and a few of us were none too happy. I had come to Seattle for one reason only and that was to win a basketball tournament.

The next morning, I stood in the doorway of my hotel room, duffle bag in hand, waiting for my roommates to finish packing their stuff. Our head coach, Jeff Oseth, walked in, and I prayed that he didn't know that those guys had been out. He told everyone to hurry up, but before he could walk out, he opened the door of a "mini fridge" in the room and pulled out a case of beer. "Is this yours?" he shouted, staring right at me. "No, no, it's not," I stammered. I kept trying to think of where it had come from, as my roommates must've brought it back during the night when I was sleeping. He slammed the fridge door shut and stormed out of the room.

Distractions aside, our tournament wouldn't go so well, as we played Central Washington in game one in front of a raucous, packed house. CWU pressed the whole game, and we committed 38 turnovers to their 28! It was a wild, sloppy game, and we lost 95–78. At one point, one of the upperclassmen looked at me, shoulders shrugged, and said, "Man, I gotta get my mind right." Maybe get some sleep before the next game, and your mind *and* body might perform a bit better.

The rest of the season was a grind. We finished the year with a total of four wins, and although we lost several close games, we were a couple years away from competing with the top teams in the Northern Sun Conference.

# 6

# MAKING THE TEAM

Following the season, I knew I wanted to transfer, not because of basketball, but because I couldn't thrive in a rural environment like Crookston. I would lay in bed at night and think, *Can I achieve my dreams here?* I narrowed my options down to the University of Wisconsin Madison and Marquette University before finally deciding on Marquette. Marquette would give me the chance to be in a fast-paced, urban environment, and I knew that I could get a top-notch education there. Basketball was still important to me, but I didn't have the talent to play at Marquette, and I figured my best shot to stay close to the game was to be a team manager. I sent a letter to Coach Tom Crean with my intentions, and surprisingly, he responded and told me to get in touch with Brian Wardle to work some summer basketball camps. Wardle had starred at Marquette and was now the Director of Basketball Operations. This was a nice opportunity for me to be around the program, meet the players and staff, and make some extra money during the summer. Given my past summer jobs, how could I not be excited about the opportunity to make money at a basketball camp?

I signed on, and it seemed like I was one of the only coaches who took the position seriously. Most of the camp coaches had been working the camp for years, and they enjoyed coming down every summer and reuniting with the Marquette staff, as well as the other coaches. As much as they were there to assist with the camp, it became obvious early on that many of these coaches were from powerful high school programs that churned out top talent each year. To call them "camp staff" was somewhat inappropriate, as they were more like honored guests. A positive experience for them could often be the difference in a recruit pledging their services to Marquette. My situation was different because I felt like I had something to prove. I worked hard at camp, brought some innovative drills to my stations, and did my best to teach the kids something. Coach Jeff Strohm, an assistant at Marquette, told me he really appreciated the fact that I ran my drills until the buzzer sounded and didn't bail out with ten seconds left on the clock. After two weeks of camp, I felt comfortable being in Milwaukee and was proud of the effort I had made to network with as many people as possible.

During the third and final week of camp, something happened to me that I will never forget. Brian Wardle would often play pick-up games with the camp staff following our last session. This was a great way to stay in shape, play competitively, and take advantage of the McGuire Center facilities, which were immaculate compared to where I had come from. As the games wound down for the evening, Brian came over to me, talked to me for a bit, and then asked if I would ever consider walking-on to next year's team. This was a complete shocker to me, as I knew the team roster was set. However, apparently Tony Gries and Jared Sichting, both walk-ons from the year before, had decided not to come back. A roster spot was open, and Wardle said that I had a month to get in shape before individual workouts start in September.

Working out during the middle of August in central Wisconsin is brutal. There were days when I simply wanted to quit, give up the dream, and enjoy the final month of summer with my friends. During my freshman year at Crookston, I had come home for two days over Christmas, but that was it the entire year. I didn't get a month-long Christmas break like every other college freshman or much of a chance to connect with family or friends. I was admittedly forced to grow up faster than I wanted to, and it was hard. I went back and forth a bit and constantly reminded myself: if this was something you really wanted, you either had to be 100% committed or bow out. As I weighed the pros and cons, the other half of me knew that playing basketball for Marquette University was a dream. A real dream that had been a part of my upbringing. From a young age, I spent weeknights watching Marquette basketball games with my dad. I remembered coaches like Kevin O'Neill and Mike Deane, and while my friends pretended to be Michael Jordan out on the driveway, I emulated former Marquette guards, Anthony Pieper and Aaron Hutchins. I didn't want to just play college basketball; I wanted to play for Marquette.

In addition to the camps, I would do random manual labor jobs back home to make money. While I got paid for the camps, I worked out an agreement with my dad to help pay for my tuition, as I was going from a virtually free education at Crookston to a very expensive one! In my eyes, every dollar counted.

To make a few extra bucks, I accepted an opportunity to "pick rock" at a farm outside of Marshfield. Essentially, myself and four other guys were tasked to walk up and down fields of soil and hand pick rocks to better prepare the land for future farming projects. The rocks came in all shapes and sizes and seemed to be littered everywhere. It was tough work in humid, ninety-five-degree heat, but I agreed because I needed the money. In one of the most bizarre things I have ever witnessed, one of the other guys had been smoking, undenounced to his father who owned the farm. When he saw his dad coming, he set the cigarette on a wooden post, which marked the southeast corner of the property. His dad pulled up on a tractor, asked us a few questions, and almost in slow motion turned around to a post that had ignited in flames. "What in the hell!" he shouted, clearly upset. We rushed to get some water and put it out. To this day, I still wonder if he ever found out the true cause of that fire?

I came home that night, and my family got a good laugh out of my story. Often, after dinner, I'd go shoot baskets on our driveway, not so much to practice but more to just clear my head and reflect on my day. As the sun started to set, it became crystal clear that I had a once in a lifetime opportunity in front of me. The other guys out in that field were good, hard-working guys, that had all attended my high school. In so many ways, we were cut from the same cloth, but they weren't getting an opportunity to chase their dreams at the highest level. As the sun finally disappeared, I tossed my basketball into a bin in my garage and told myself that tomorrow was "go time."

My grandpa passed away a couple weeks before I had started the workouts at the age of 83. Cletus Willkom was a Captain in the Army and served in Italy during World War 2. He was awarded a purple heart for injuries sustained in battle and a bronze star for heroism in battle when he assisted a wounded soldier to safety at point-blank range.

A couple years prior, my grandpa told me a story about his time in Italy. The squadron had been hiking for several days in the mountains. As they made their way along their route, they stumbled upon a large cave and decided that this would be a good place to rest for the evening. After a night there, the group headed south, while another squadron of U.S. soldiers took over the cave. The next night, the cave was ambushed, and every man in there was killed. Avoiding eye contact and looking off to the side, my grandpa, in a rushed, but matter of fact voice, concluded, "And I still feel bad about that." He stood up and walked away, as if to imply that that was enough for one day, and despite the questions that loomed in my mind, I respected that.

After the war, my grandpa married my grandma at the Quonset Point Naval Air Station in Rhode Island. After they were married, both having traveled around the world in the military, they decided to move home to Cadott, WI, a town of 1400 people and start a family. My grandpa dedicated the rest of his life to dentistry and was proud to have served generations of families in the community.

A few days before my grandpa passed, my family went up to visit him at the hospital, and he looked like a million bucks. If we hadn't been in a hospital, I would've never known he was sick. The usual conversation began between my parents and him, but he wasn't having it. In fact, almost immediately, he started talking about how he was working to get in shape. The man was old and about to meet his maker, and yet, on that day, my grandpa rolled off his bed and started doing calf-raises on the side of the bed. After a few reps, he crawled back into the covers and looked at me. "You compete hard," he instructed. That was the last time I saw him. Foreshadowing is a potent literary tool, but this story aside, my grandpa knew what I was about to go through. Pain would be a daily commonality for me over the next ten months, and yet, I knew my grandpa was looking down on me, believing that I could do it.

As football practice rolled around that August, I had basically established a new residence at Our Lady of Peace gymnasium, a small, Catholic, grade school gym, that was home to my first competitive basketball game as a fourth-grader. Joe Konieczny, my former coach, friend, and overall mentor, had given me a key to the gym when he found out I would be given an opportunity to try out for the Marquette men's basketball team. Looking me squarely in the eye and with a serious look on his face, he handed me the key and simply said, "Go get em," implying a vote of confidence but also a subtle, *Please take advantage of this opportunity.* Joe had been the older brother I never had: a guy with good morals and values that always seemed to guide me in the right direction. Making the team was my goal, but I wanted it just as bad for Joe, who had spent thousands of hours with me since the seventh grade, pushing me as a basketball player and as a man. He deserved to see one of his guys "make it."

As I went back to work, I told myself, *You've done all of this before.* For the past ten years, I had been putting myself through similar workouts. The difference now, though, was that I had extra motivation; I could literally feel it in my gut. My morning session was the toughest, as it consisted of a series of ball-handling workouts, followed by some finishing drills, jump shots off the dribble, and ended with a full court finishing series. The workout usually lasted about ninety minutes, but this was ninety minutes in a gym with no air conditioning by myself. Occasionally, I would have company, with the janitor or school faculty checking in to see what I was up to. Other than that, though, I found it extremely difficult to find other people to work out with because nobody in their right mind wanted to put themselves through what I was about to go through for the next thirty days.

Following the morning sessions, I would grab lunch at home and then head to the Marshfield YMCA for a strength and conditioning program. I would lift weights three times per week, while the other two days were focused on hill sprints, agility drills, and plyometrics. Most Division 1 athletes have phenomenal athletic ability, and I knew that I would have to improve every day if I were to have a chance to compete with these guys. I'd head down to the water treatment plant and run hill sprints until I couldn't run anymore. About half way through August, I started running them in a weight vest, and I'd add weight each week. By the end of the month, I was running with more than 40 lbs. strapped to that vest. It was humid. It was hot. At one point, someone got out of their car and came running over after they saw me lying on my back at the top of that hill, barely able to breathe, but thankful to have run one more that day than I did the day before. My thumbs up slowed their stride, and after a brief conversation, they returned to their car.

Evenings were a nice opportunity to give my legs a rest and get some shots up on The Gun, an electronic shooting machine that rebounds the basketballs for you. I was never a great shooter, but I worked hard at it in hopes that I could effectively compete in college-level perimeter workouts. Our Lady of Peace had one in their back closet, which is probably still a secret to people in Marshfield, but I wore that thing out on a nightly basis.

After thirty straight days, I was headed to Marquette, not as a basketball player, but as a student like everyone else. I think my parents were worried that I had become so obsessed with basketball that my academics would take a back seat. Deep down, I knew what I was doing. School was first, and I was going to Marquette to become the best student and friend that I could be. If basketball fit into that picture, I would be ecstatic. Of course, that was the message I had to project externally. When I looked myself in the mirror and evaluated my own heart, I fully expected to make the team. No one could rob me of the time and effort that I had just put in. Like so many times before, I told myself, *You're good enough.* More importantly, I had put myself in a position to have a shot, which is all I ever wanted.

Because I was a transfer student, I was assigned to live in the Haggerty House, which was an all-male transfer house of twenty-six residents. The House, on the corner of 16th and Kilbourne, had formerly been home to a fraternity that lost it after a few too many "keggers." At first, I wasn't too thrilled about living with twenty-five guys, but it was a blessing in the end, as we essentially formed an informal brotherhood, minus the parties. Chris Teff, a teammate of mine at Minnesota Crookston, was my roommate, along with Nick Niedermann, a random roommate from Delafield, WI. Chris was also attempting to walk-on, and it was great having someone around that shared my vision.

Brian Wardle had said that he would contact us the third week of school. Coach Crean had been busy dealing with Brandon Bell's transfer (Bell had gotten kicked off the team for marijuana), while the rest of the team was knee-deep in workouts. Upon Wardle's call, I had no idea what to expect, as the workout was scheduled for a Saturday morning, and I was going home to visit my family following the session. I showed up well-rested, well-hydrated, and ready to go, but what would go down over the next couple hours was the reason the public doesn't witness private workouts.

I had been in the Al McGuire Center (AL) on several occasions during my time as a camp coach in the summer. That morning, though, was different, as I was led down a side set of stairs that was accessible only by key card. At the bottom of the stairs were the doors to the Marquette weight room on the right, followed by two double doors straight ahead that led into the Kasten practice gym. The gym had banners on all four sides of the walls, showing love to the Marquette All-Americans and those that had or were currently playing in the NBA. It was a motivating environment, with no windows, and an upper catwalk where student managers would video tape workouts and practices.

The workout was based on one premise that the coaching staff laid out before we began: "We want you to quit. The faster you drop out, say you can't, or just give up, the faster we can move on with our lives." Rob Hanley, Chris Teff, and I were the chosen three. Jason Rabedeaux, Jeff Strohm, and Brian Wardle, all Marquette coaches, were on hand to run the workout, while Coach Crean was positioned on the sideline to watch. I was nervous at first, but after a few minutes, I would need to focus on breathing because their wouldn't be any breaks.

The drills were intense and were one right after the other, followed by sprint after sprint after sprint. We were lucky when we were "awarded" a "22," which was a four-length sprint baseline to baseline in under twenty-two seconds. If all three guys didn't make it in time, we would run again and so on. Unfortunately, the majority of our sprints were "17's," which are seventeen sideline to sideline sprints in under a minute. The rules were the same as the 22. Most basketball players can finish a 17 in under a minute, but try finishing it following a game of full court 1 on 1, up to seven by ones. Mental toughness is putting everything you have into winning that game, losing, and then having to finish the sprint in under a minute. To be completely honest, most rational people, if down by a conceivable deficit, would save up their energy at the end of the game so they could finish the sprint. Getting to that "never quit, never say die" mentality is a subtle difference between champions and their competition.

We did a three-point shooting drill at the end, and I actually air-balled one of my attempts, as I could hardly feel my arms and legs. What would've normally been viewed as embarrassing was almost the signal to every assistant coach that they had done their job. Everything we did that day had a winner. It became real clear that Marquette was about winning basketball games, and winning basketball games was the result of winning every drill, every sprint, and every loose ball during practice.

I left that workout questioning my desire to be on the team. If today's workout was the daily protocol, I knew I would never make it. My body was sore and dehydrated, and mentally, I felt a bit dejected: *I trained as hard as I could for two months, and I still feel like this?* Yet, as I processed what had just taken place, I was proud of the way I competed. Everyone in that gym did everything they could to make me quit, and yet I was still standing. And, after a relaxing weekend at home, I couldn't wait for the next one.

With the official start of practice less than a month away, the Marquette coaching staff was extremely busy putting things into place for the upcoming season. Yet, they still had time to put me through three more individual workouts. When I say individual workouts, there would be three to four guys participating. Each one was just as hard as the first, and we had a guy quit during our third session because he was "sick."

My second workout was one that sticks out in my memory because my future roommate and close friend, Marc Dettmann, was one of the participants. Marc was a nice guy who was always working at out at the rec center and was one of the few people I could call a friend since my arrival at Marquette. Marc had been a standout basketball and soccer player at Marquette University High School in Milwaukee (WI). When we arrived at the workout, we were both surprised to see one another, but I was happy Marc was getting the same opportunity I was to make the team. After several drills and sprints, Wardle brought us together and explained the rules of full court 1 on 1, in which he emphasized that we had to guard each other the length of the floor. Every basketball player knows that playing full court defense is downright grueling, but like previous workouts, I wasn't in any position to call the shots. We played first guy up to four baskets, which can take an extended amount of time when guys are already fatigued. My strategy was simple: beat Marc up the court offensively and turn him as many times as I could defensively. I figured if I could wear him out bringing the ball up the floor, fatigue would prohibit him from getting a good shot off. The drill began, and Coach Strohm yelled to stay low and move my feet. In situations like these, it doesn't matter if Marc was my best friend in the world. Friendships are forgotten, and winning is all that matters in the Al McGuire Kasten practice gym. After a couple of physical trips down the floor, it was my turn on offense, and I capitalized with a couple of nice moves to the basket. Words of encouragement from the coaching staff overshadowed the fatigue that had set in, and following a couple hard fought exchanges, I banked in a shot from the left side of the lane to win the drill. Marc ran his sprints, and I encouraged him because I respected the hell out of him for the way he competed. To this day, I wonder if Marc would have made the team had we not been paired in the same workout? To Marc's credit, he walked-on to the men's soccer team as a senior and won the starting goalie position. Not bad for a senior walk-on and certainly a credit to Marc's hard work and persistence as an athlete. Marc would become one of my roommates during my junior and senior years and later one of the groomsmen in my wedding.

After my fourth workout, I was getting anxious because I had given the staff everything I had four times, and yet, no decision had been made as to who would join that year's team. Following the fourth workout, the staff was holding a campuswide walk-on event for anyone that wanted to attend. Essentially, the tryout consisted of a few drills, followed by a series of 5 on 5 pick-up games. Wardle had indicated that I would participate in both, although the individual workout had taken a lot out of me. As I limped my way into the MU locker room to get some water and mentally prepare for another two hours, Coach Crean entered the locker room. Expecting him to go into the back-locker area, I hardly acknowledged him, but to my surprise, he took a seat on the couch in the player's lounge area. "Hell of a workout fellas," he said to Chris Teff and myself. "You know what," he continued, "you guys don't have to go back out there." As he finished his sentence, Wardle busted through the door and intensely indicated for us to get back into the gym. Crean, hesitating for a second, finally told Brian that we didn't have to go back. It was then, at that moment, that I finally felt a sense of acknowledgment for what I had done the past few weeks. On four different occasions, I worked out to the point of utter exhaustion with little to no feedback. Although nothing was official yet, it was certainly a good sign for Coach Crean to acknowledge our hard work, and I left the gym that night thinking that maybe, just maybe, I was going to be a part of something special.

That night, Wardle asked us to write a one-page letter to Coach Crean explaining why we should be on the team. After contemplating what I should say, I realized that my message should be simple and to the point. My entire life up to that point had been characterized by hard work and unselfishness; a letter outlining anything else wouldn't be authentic. I also wanted to drive home my passion for Marquette basketball. This was more than just trying to make a college team. Marquette basketball had been a major part of my life up to that point, and I could honestly say that wearing the MU uniform meant more to me than anyone else vying for a spot.

The next day, Chris Teff and I had a meeting with Coach Crean, and he asked us about the sincerity of the letters. I had nothing to hide, and the meeting was a great way for me to reaffirm my position in a face to face setting. By that time, Coach Crean certainly knew a lot about me, both as a basketball player and as a competitor. He had witnessed the workouts, watched me play and coach at summer camps, and even watched me compete against his guys during an open scrimmage. After voicing my two cents, he was very passionate that we understand the rules and expectations of anyone in the program. Being around the Al McGuire Center the past few weeks had given me a taste of what was expected, but it was still good to hear these from the boss. Rule number one was simple: "The program owes you nothing." There would be no special treatment, and Coach Crean vowed to coach us like every other guy on the team. Every mistake would be criticized, every shot analyzed, and so forth. "I am going to coach you," he said, "and if you don't want to be coached, then please tell me now." Next, he emphasized that we wouldn't be allowed to make any off the court mistakes. "It is an honor and a privilege to be a part of this storied program, and you will never forget that." I had never had any off the court problems before, and this was a very reasonable expectation. If I were a coach, I would expect the same thing out of my players. Finally, he said, "I want you to push these guys; make them work." With that, he said, "I'll see you tomorrow ready to go."

# 7

# STRENGTH &
# CONDITIONING

Midnight Madness was something that I attended as a kid, and it acts as the official start to the college basketball season. The team is introduced, along with a dunk and three-point shooting contest, followed by a team scrimmage. Coach had given me my roster spot on Friday morning, and Midnight Madness would begin later that evening. As much as I would have liked to participate, I understood Crean's stance as to holding Chris and I out. We hadn't been a part of pre-season conditioning with the team, and it wouldn't be fair to reward a couple guys who hadn't accomplished anything yet. In addition, because both of us had been on scholarship at Minnesota Crookston, we were required to sit out the season per NCAA rules because we had transferred from a scholarship school to a scholarship school. Sitting behind the bench, I watched intently as the guys did some drill work to open the session. Every missed lay-up was fifteen push-ups, whether we were behind closed doors or in front of four thousand people. And I'm not talking just normal lay-ups: these were highly contested shots, with a coach often guarding the dribbler, along with another coach waiting near the basket with a blocking pad.

The assistant coaches were barking demands, and the players

as a unit were extremely vocal. By the end of the season, it was crystal clear that one of Coach Crean's biggest pet peeves was a quiet gym. There would be no silent leaders at Marquette, and every guy was responsible for bringing a vocal energy to practice. In fact, sensational practices by guys like Dameon Mason or Joe Chapman were often overshadowed by their lack of talking. If a guy took a charge or made a steal, the gym would erupt with chatter and applause.

After midnight madness had concluded, I headed back to the Haggerty House, intent on getting a good night's rest. By that time, I had called my family and friends back home, and they were ecstatic upon hearing the news. One of my first calls was to Joe Konieczny, who two months earlier had challenged me to put in the work. As much as that month back in Marshfield mattered, this was the culmination of a lifetime of dedication to the game. As happy as I was to share this with them, it was bittersweet knowing that most would never know what I went through to get there. People in Marshfield would talk about the hometown kid who made the team, the neighbor that made the team, the parishioner that made the team, the coworker that made the team, but they would never understand what it took. They would share in my joy, but they would never share in my pain or fatigue following day-long exploits at the gym, on the hill, or in that weight vest. I guess that's why it means so much when people close to you find success in whatever they do. While you share the success, the true satisfaction comes from both understanding the trials and tribulations that led up to that point. The next day would be my first in a Marquette uniform, and I couldn't have been more excited to get started.

I showed up to the locker room an hour early. The entry door was accessible by a four-digit code, and upon entry, there was a player's lounge, with a large TV, couches, and Gatorade machine. Moving through the lounge, the actual locker room was the next room to the left. My locker was wedged in the corner, next to Dameon Mason's and Steve Novak's. Already hanging there was a name plate, a Nike practice jersey with the number #10 on it, Nike practice shorts, Wigwam socks, Nike shoes, and even a pair of Marquette basketball spandex that had the logo on the waistband. I have been around a few college programs in my life, and I must admit that Marquette really went the extra mile with the custom underwear. Anything to gain an edge.

To start every practice, strength coach Scott Holsopple would take the team through a dynamic stretching routine using bands. We'd do various leg swings, and I looked over at some of the scholarship guys to make sure I was doing the right stretches.

My first couple practices went really well and were far less grueling than what I had been through in the individual workouts. It was fun having a whole team there to support you, and I'll never forget Coach Crean during the first week of practice. There was a renewed enthusiasm that comes from starting with a blank slate. Every season is a journey: bonds are formed and tears are shed, as every member of the team, from the coaching staff to the student managers, works to maximize the collective potential of the group. The passion and excitement in his voice was unparallel to anything I had ever seen before. 5 on 5 sets or new defensive packages that were slow to materialize were going to work, and any doubt by the players was immediately replaced by a reassuring Crean, who was as much a psychologist, as he was a coach. Post practice speeches at most programs sound something like this: "Good job today. We need to work on this, this, and this. We'll see you tomorrow." At Marquette, Crean wanted us to see the big picture. "We *are* going to win," he said. "You guys need to be competitors in everything you do. Whether it's in basketball or business, you need to want to kick people's ass."

On Monday, Chris Teff, Rob Hanley, and I would have our first strength and conditioning session with strength coach, Scott Holsopple. Rob was our third walk-on and was a freshman from Waukesha Catholic Memorial (WI). Going back to Scott, the man stood about 5'8", was built square to the ground, and always wore sweatpants. He had been an All-American boxer at Penn State University and worked there as a strength coach before arriving at Marquette. The session was scheduled for 6:00 a.m., and none of us knew what to expect. We figured he would put us through a variety of exercises to see how strong we were and set up a program thereafter based on those numbers. Chris and I were in bed by ten o'clock that night, as first impressions were important, and I wanted to be ready to perform at a high level.

I awoke the next morning to my radio alarm, put on my sweats, and had a good breakfast in my dorm room. It's hard to explain how excited I was to go work with Scott. You'd hear stories about how tough he was, how hard he pushed guys, that "Marquette Toughness" had come from Scott Holsopple. Holsopple's work couldn't have been more visible than with Dwyane Wade, who arrived as skinny, 185 lb. kid and left as a 210 lb. sculpted machine.

As I made my way to the weight room, I was about 95% excited and 5% fearful about what might go on for the next hour or so. From the very second I walked through the door, Scott didn't like me or anyone else for that matter. In fact, he didn't say a nice thing to me for the next five months. We started with chin-ups, followed by dips and the legendary leg press. There were pictures in the weight room of guys on the leg press, and they weren't pretty. In fact, some of the pictures just showed guys sprawled out on the floor, which I would come to learn was a common result of the exercise. For every photo that adorns a team media guide, these were the photos that made it all come to life. There would be days the rest of the year when I would be walking by the weight room, and I could always tell if someone was on the leg press because I could hear the screams from outside. Each exercise that we did didn't have a predetermined amount of repetitions. You were expected to do as many reps as you could and then squeeze out a few more with the help of a partner. Sounds easy enough, right?

After a few sets of chins and dips, I was locked in to the leg press ready to go. After about five reps, I had nothing left because he had loaded the thing with an insane amount of weight. I figured I could maybe get one more with my partner's help. Scott, perched over the leg press like a lion viewing his prey, said, "You need to get twenty to get out." He didn't say to try to get one more, or even try for ten, but twenty. At that point, I physically didn't think I could do it; I simply wasn't strong enough. I honestly felt like crying because each rep was more painful than anything I had ever done before, and there was a realistic chance that all this weight was going to come crashing down on me because my legs were going to snap. After loud screams and giving everything, I had made it to ten. It was a blessing just to get to double digits, but the reality was that I had ten remaining, and Scott wasn't budging. One by one, I was yelling and pushing with every ounce of energy in my body. "Twelve," he yelled, followed by, "Willkom's going to waste the rest of my day, damnit!" After number 13, I honestly wanted to quit. My legs were shaking, my face was white, and I thought about how good my life had been before I walked in to meet Scott. Looking around, there was no one to bail me out or make me feel better. There was no predetermined time on a clock that would release me from Scott's watch. This was between me and the machine. 14. *I can't do it.* 15. *My legs are going to freaking explode.* 16. *Just get me the hell out of here.* 17. *I can't do it.* 18. *Just give up.* 19. *Get tough.* 20. After my 20th rep, I thought, *This was the hardest thing I had ever done.* I couldn't believe it was over, that I had actually finished! As I waggled out of the machine, I tried to take a step, but I crumbled back to the floor like a rag doll. I literally collapsed. My legs were numb, and my head pounded from pushing so hard. I felt like I was going to throw up, which was shocking to me because I had never thrown up from working out, ever.

When the other two guys finished the leg press and had similar experiences, I couldn't wait to walk out that door and relax my mind and body. I was mentally taxed and physically numb, but it was over. Scott, on the other hand, looked at the three of us with a smile on his face and excitedly proclaimed, "You guys are going to puke today!" He didn't say "good job" or make even an ounce of effort to affirm what had just been done. A message was clearly being sent in the fewest words possible.

Following his statement, he led us over to the VersaClimber machine, and now it was obvious that the workout wasn't over. The VersaClimber is a climbing machine that has two straps for your feet and a handle for each hand. In a standing position, as one arm goes up, the opposite foot goes down. Scott told us that we had to climb 3,000 feet in twenty minutes to be done. I had never been on a VersaClimber machine before, but I knew this was going to be hard. After about ten minutes, it was starting to look like I wasn't going to make it unless I really picked up my speed. My shoulders ached, and my calves were numb. I kept thinking about my family, my Grandpa Willkom that had passed, and how hard I had worked to get to this point. It wasn't about physical strength at that point because I didn't have any. I had to forget all of that, and closing my eyes so I couldn't see the timer, I gave it everything I had, one step at a time. I looked up to the sound of a beeping timer, indicating that my twenty minutes was up. My score? 3,002 feet, which was literally two steps above the target. Two steps! Just like that, it was over. We were free to leave, and yet none of us could even move. Scott had done his job.

It was 7:00 a.m., and I had my first class of the day in an hour. I thought to myself, *There's no way I was only in there for an hour*, as it had felt like a lifetime. At the same time, my head was hurting so bad that I was having diffulties thinking about where to go next. I could've sat in the locker room all day because my body was about to die, but this was the life of a student-athlete. My classes went from 8:00-12:00 on Monday, Wednesday, and Friday. At 1:30, practice would begin, and occasionally we would have film sessions at night to talk about various offensive sets. To top it off, we had a board in our locker room called "Maximize the Day," which allowed you to write in the "extra work" that you had put in early in the morning before strength & conditioning or late at night after film. I love the concept in theory, but who in the hell had time for "extra work?!" The one thing that you learn in a hurry is that Coach Crean or any coach for that matter couldn't care less what you did in strength and conditioning earlier that day. They expect the best from you from the moment you walk on the floor. As I mentioned earlier, each missed layup during practice was fifteen push-ups. Push-ups were the last thing I wanted to do after finally getting loose following my rigorous workout earlier in the day. But, it wasn't about what I wanted to do. It was Coach Crean's way or Coach Crean's way, and I was reminded of that more than once. Following that first day, I was scared to even look at Scott. I still couldn't believe what I had gone through, and it wasn't something you could explain to other people because they had never been through anything even comparable. I did know one thing, though: I would see Scott in about thirty-six hours at 6:00 a.m., and the thought alone made me sick.

From day one, I knew Travis Diener could play, but I didn't realize how good this guy was until I saw him do the same things every day. Travis was our starting point guard and had averaged 18 points and 6 assists per game as a junior, earning first-team Conference USA honors. This was his team as a senior, and our success would largely depend on his ability to get others up to his level. During a practice early in the season, Jeff Strohm was all over me to stop him. Coach Crean was working on a couple of post-up sets for Travis, and from a coaching perspective, it seemed like I was doing everything I could to contain him. Every catch was a battle, and I knew I had an advantage if I could make him catch it close to the three-point line. After the catch, I did a good job of not allowing him to back me down, and every shot was contested with a hand up. Despite my textbook post defense, Travis was hitting shots that I had never seen guys make in a competitive situation. Fade away bank shots from either shoulder, step back high-arcing shots, three-pointers with my forearm on his hip. It was frustrating to guard against moves that were unguardable, but that is what made Travis an NBA player. For guys that are limited athletically or don't have proto-type size, they need to be able to make shots that the opposition can't defend. People ask me all the time, "What made Travis so good?" What separated Travis from everybody else was his ability to hit contested shots and make moves against a live defender. Kids today constantly work out in 1 on 0 situations, with an occasional mock defender thrown into the mix. I didn't watch Travis work out as a kid nor do I know what types of drills he did to develop his game. However, I can bet that a lot of live 1 on 1 was involved once he developed a consistent shooting form. Basketball is about reading the defense, and yet so often kids are trained to be able to hit shots from spots, regardless of how the defense is positioned. In fact, former Gonzaga superstar Adam Morrison was once asked how he worked on his game: "Game shots, game spots, game speed," he said. He couldn't have been more right, except he forgot to mention a live defender. If you are an aspiring basketball player, work on making plays against a defender with only a dribble or two. Recognize how the defense is playing you and incorporate your skills into a competitive situation.

We'd often run live 5 on 5 sets, and if Travis missed a three to finish the play, Crean would always kick it back out to him for another shot. On more than a hundred occasions, I don't think he missed a second three-point attempt from the same spot.

If you are not tough, both mentally and physically, you will never survive at Marquette. I had heard about the loose ball scuffles that regularly occurred during MU practices, but it wasn't until I was involved in one that I realized the insanity that occurred during a 50/50 ball. It was still early in the season, and hustle plays are a great way to earn the respect of your teammates. One day in practice, a ball was deflected during a 5 on 5 drill, and I knew that I had to get that ball. Exploding out of my stance, I dove after it and was subsequently engaged by a swarm of blue jerseys. A loose ball at Marquette is like a fumble on the football field: even if you have no chance to get the ball, you better at least pile on in support of your team. About a minute passed, and the guys that realized they didn't have a chance disengaged from the scramble, leaving only Joe Chapman and I fighting for the ball. Joe stood 6'4" and weighed 220 lbs., outweighing me by about sixty pounds. Motivated to earn respect and simply my competitive nature, I held on for dear life. Trying to rip the ball away, guys began to hoot and holler, cheering us on. Just as I thought I had an advantage and was about to come away with it, Joe began to elbow my head into the wood floor. At that point, I remember thinking, *No matter what, don't let go*. As psychotic as it sounds, I continued, amid the words of encouragement from my teammates. Finally, after the blows to the head had become unbearable, I surrendered the ball. Leaving practice that day, I had quite a headache as I walked through campus, thinking about what it might feel like to have a concussion. I had battled Joe to the brink of defeat, and even in losing, was helped off the floor by my teammates, who softly offered words of encouragement and consolation. I lay down that night thinking about the way everything had played out. Another move here or there, and I would've had him, and yet, I was proud of myself for not backing down. Respect is something that you earn, and that day would prove significant in our journey to become a team.

A couple days had passed, and it was time to see Scott again in the weight room. Saying we all weren't intimidated was like saying Madison isn't the capitol of Wisconsin. Fear is an interesting part of life, because as Coach Crean reiterated on multiple occasions, "It can either motivate you or paralyze you." In my case, I had experienced thoughts of failure during my first session with Scott. Thoughts of *I can't* or *Impossibility* entered my brain on a frequent basis, especially during the leg press. Yet, failure couldn't be an option for me, otherwise I could spend my afternoons serving hamburgers in Schroeder dining hall. Surpassing a mental roadblock is extremely difficult, and yet, all of us have them. How many people stop at ten repetitions simply because their workout sheet says ten? Could you do twelve, maybe fourteen? Pushing ourselves to our absolute maximum rarely occurs, if ever, but Scott Holsopple would take me where I had never been.

The second workout was more upper body, a lot of chin-ups and dips, followed by my favorite (I'm kidding) exercise, which was manual neck. Since the head is the heaviest part of the body, Scott was a firm believer in having a strong neck. Consequently, he would do manual neck exercises with each of us individually, where he would provide resistance with his hands, and we would move our heads back and forth, both on our backs and on our stomachs. I had never felt like I was going to get my head ripped off before, but, motivated by the movie Braveheart, I persevered through the twenty repetitions.

Later that day in my 8:00 a.m. accounting class with Mr. Dole, I could hardly stay awake. Credits and debits sounded like a Beethoven symphony to me, and despite my desire to learn the material, I simply could not keep my head up. The person sitting next to me kept tapping me, "John, John," she said. I needed to stay awake during that class. But, as I attempted to lift my head off the table, I simply couldn't move my neck. Let me tell you, being tired is one thing. But not being able to move your head is a phenomenon that I hope none of you will ever experience. Luckily, class concluded, and I was energized to leave by the barrage of students packing up their books. I would go on to have a great semester of accounting and even consider it as a major at the advice of Mr. Dole. To this day, had he asked me why my head was stuck on the table, I would have told him the truth.

# 8

# SCRIMMAGES

Aside from the players and coaches, Marquette has a tremendous marketing department that is responsible for creating a positive image of Marquette basketball not only in Milwaukee, but also the United States. The entire team is brought in for individual pictures with our uniforms on, and programs, trading cards, flyers, and videos are produced. In-game videos on the Jumbotron are filmed in the pre-season, and a buzz is created before the team even steps on the floor for the first time. Mike Broeker did a tremendous job of binding together the legacy of past Marquette teams with the excitement of the current squad. Marquette basketball is recognized across the country, and the marketing department is a big reason for that.

A couple weeks into the season, Marquette had scheduled an intersquad scrimmage that would be open to the public. The teams were split up evenly, although having Travis on my team was a sure bet if I were a gambling man. A full crowd came out to see the team play in a live game situation for the first time since Midnight Madness. Coaches, players, and managers were all excited because it was beginning to feel like basketball season. The cool, fall air welcomed fans to the four-thousand-seat Al McGuire Center, while we were busy getting taped and stretched in the corridors below.

The ball was tipped, and a few minutes into the game, I would get my first taste of playing in front of the MU faithful. For me, being on the floor meant playing great defense, taking care of the basketball, and executing 5 on 5 sets in the half-court. I knew it was important to Coach Crean that we experiment with different offensive sets because any coach wants to see how things work during live, unscripted contests. A few minutes in, Travis hit me on the left wing, and I banked in a fifteen-footer. Yes, I meant to bank it. In fact, I had attempted more bank shots in the past two weeks than ever in my life. If you've followed the career of Dwyane Wade, you would have noticed that bank shooting was something he perfected at Marquette. Every day towards the end of practice, we would shoot ten-foot bank shots from both wings, having to make a certain amount in a designated time period. Shooting off the glass requires concentration, especially at the end of practices when guys don't have their legs. So, hitting that bank shot was a culmination of two weeks of work for me, and I'll never forget my first two points in a Marquette uniform.

Led by Dameon Mason's 26 points, our blue squad took home the inaugural Friday night event. It certainly felt great to win, but it felt even better to be spared the conditioning session that was put upon the losing Gold team the next morning. Members of the media, fans, and students evaluate preseason scrimmages like Rick Majerus staring at a steak. It's their first chance to see the team after months away from the game, especially at a non-football school like Marquette. Yet, these same "supporters" don't have to condition every time they lose a sale, show up late to a meeting, or perform below their best. Imagine being held to a standard of perfection at 19-years-old, with every mistake analyzed, and every loss punished. The mental toughness of college athletes isn't built by winning: it's perfected by losing.

Practice was great on that Saturday. Games, especially games that don't count, are refreshing for everyone, and Friday's contest was no different. Following Saturday's practice, everyone stayed after to film each of our pre-season 5 on 5 sets. Travis would run with the starters, and I would run the point for the second group. I remembered most of the sets, which is a feat considering we had close to fifty on top of my eighteen credit hours of school. Even though I would never play in a game, I studied that tape closely over the next few days. As a point guard on any team, there is an obligation to know where every guy needs to be, whether you're an all-star or the third string guy on the end of the bench. To those who don't think sports translate to the real world, I certainly learned a great lesson about taking pride in my job. If watching tape was what it took to do my job well, then I was going to watch tape. To this day, I still have a copy of that tape, and unfortunately, it's not a popular choice when deciding what to watch on a Saturday night! And yet for me, that tape represents so much more than the footage in that video. Memories re-emerge, and I can visualize myself on the McGuire Center floor; the sounds, the smells, the aura of a place that I dreamed about as a kid. It was the Anthony Piepers, Chris Crawfords, Tony Millers, Damon Keys: guys that paved the way for such a magical facility to be built. And there I was, wearing number ten, with full appreciation and gratitude for what those guys meant to the program.

The following week, another public scrimmage was held, only this time, I ended up on the losing end. Saturday morning conditioning is like waking up on Christmas and having to go to work: you just feel awful about it. The weight room at the McGuire Center was beautiful, painted in blue and gold, and contained some of the best equipment I had ever seen. Pictures of Robert Jackson and Dwyane Wade occupied the wall as you walked through the front door. Free weights, pull-up bars, sand jugs, cardio equipment, and other weight equipment gleamed, as if they had never been touched. The weight room, Kasten practice gym, training room, and Al McGuire gym were all on the bottom level of the facility that could only be accessed by key card. Players, staff, and maintenance were the only ones on campus with such access.

My alarm went off at 5:15 a.m., and I bundled up in my Marquette sweat suit, winter coat, hat, and gloves. Walking to the Al McGuire center in the dark had become almost a spiritual time for me to think and mentally prepare for the day. Often, I'd watch the snow fall, illuminated by the street lights, and think about what my goals were for the day. As I made my way down those stairs at 5:45 a.m., I heard loud screams that appeared to be coming from the weight room. Crusty-eyed and half asleep, I squinted through the glass on the door and saw Scott on the chest press by himself. Veins popping out of his head and teeth clenched, it looked like he was training for the World's Strongest Man competition. He always wore a sweatshirt, even when he lifted. If there was any question as to what was coming, the answer was crystal clear through that window.

The VersaClimber machine is a workout like no other, and since it was introduced to me in my first ever strength & conditioning session, it became something I grew to hate. The machine is built to mimic the movements of a mountain climber, with your feet in peddles and your hands placed on handle bars that extend above your head. Productivity on the machine is measured by the number of feet you climb in a set period of time. Essentially, you would gain feet by lengthening the motion of your climbs or by speeding them up. The VersaClimber was so tough because your arms stayed above your heart the entire exercise. Athletes who run or bike can rest their arms on their hips to catch their breath. Try that on the VersaClimber, and you fall off and end up on the floor. If the exercise itself doesn't sound hard enough, Scott's 3,000-foot requirement in twenty minutes was calculated to get every last ounce of effort out of you. Not only was the pace frantic, but twenty minutes for one conditioning exercise usually falls in the endurance category. Athletes in any sport can rarely perform at a high threshold for several minutes, much less twenty. That morning, I pushed myself as hard as I could and climbed 3,020 feet in the twenty minutes, which was a bit better than my first attempt. In fact, I tackled the

VersaClimber at least twenty times that year, and never did I get above 3,100 feet. To say that Scott had perfected the specifications to push us to our max was an understatement.

Athletes and businessmen, entrepreneurs and politicians, constantly talk about motivation, and how different forms of motivation have helped them reach great heights. In my case, the VersaClimber taught me the importance of mental motivation to achieve a goal. Some of my best thinking came during those twenty-minute conditioning sessions, as I would create a mental vision of my family, my grandfather that had passed, or even the girl in Mashuda Hall that I had a crush on at the time. As crazy as this sounds, my physical performance always improved when I had a strong mental focus and could block everything out around me. Days when I created an inner anger, excitement, or "prove you wrong" scenario not only made the conditioning sessions go faster, but I wasn't as exhausted in the end because my focus hadn't been on the fatigue. Having the right mindset was paramount to my success.

I know for a fact that Coach Crean was always trying to gain a mental edge by reading books or observing other coaches. Players talked about the books in his office, many of which were completely unrelated to basketball. Coach would also take time each fall to watch the Wisconsin Badger and Green Bay Packer football teams practice. Obviously, the drills and practices were different from those on the hardwood, but the lessons were learned in the preparation, communication, and attention to detail. Of course, Crean's brother in laws were John and Jim Harbaugh, so he may have just been brushing up his football acumen for the next family reunion.

A couple years after playing for Coach Crean, I attended a Milwaukee Bucks practice session at the Cousins Center and got to watch Michael Redd, Andrew Bogut, and Earl Boykins. While the talent on the floor was impressive, there was a dramatic difference in the intensity of the workout compared to the college level. While Coach Larry Krystkowiak seemed prepared, his attention to detail was lacking, and the team's effort at practice was subpar. NBA practices lack the intensity of any college workout, but from a coaching perspective, I just can't accept subpar execution. Screens need to be set properly, and guys need to be in the right spot, make the right reads, and space the floor well. This simply doesn't happen unless the coach demands it, and it all comes back to making a focused mentality habitual. Coaches, players, and trainers who know how to focus and concentrate in the moment achieve success.

# 9

# TOURNAMENT CHAMPIONS

As if we weren't already motivated with our first game just days away, Coach Crean made it a point that we would be playing in two tournaments to start the season. While we were guaranteed the games, Crean stressed that this would be a season of championships, with our first title opportunity just days away as part of the Black Coaches Association (BCA) tournament. The following week, we would be participating in the Pepsi Blue and Gold Classic tournament and would have the opportunity for a second championship trophy. Such a strategy may seem rather elementary, and that is exactly what it was. Players were reminded of their days in grade school, junior high, and high school, when playing for trophies was all that mattered. Every guy on my team had played some form of AAU basketball growing up, and while our motivations may have been different, the end goal was always to bring home a title.

Our first game in the BCA Classic matched us up with Western Carolina, who had a solid team, despite the loss of Kevin Martin to the NBA. David Berghoffer, a Middleton (WI) alum, was back at the center position, and fans always appreciate seeing a Wisconsin native out on the floor. Despite a rocky start, we won our first game

75-64, led by Travis's 27 points. A win over Illinois State took us to the championship game, where we would face Air Force, coached by Chris Mooney.

Air Force was a difficult team to prepare for because they loved to back cut for lay-ups. As a basketball fan, I always respected Pete Carril's style of play at Princeton, and Air Force ran a similar set-up, utilizing a high post man to facilitate their offense. We worked the entire week at getting our head and hands turned to see the basketball on back cuts. As a player who liked to pass the ball, it was enjoyable being encouraged to throw risky passes all week without being reprimanded for turning the ball over. In fact, I was probably yelled at more that week for not making enough "bad" passes. The coaching staff wanted our team to be ready for a pass at any given moment. If your man cut to the basket, but you couldn't see the passer, you were rewarded by getting on the line and sprinting for twenty-two seconds. The message was simple: see the ball at all times and maintain contact with your man. While our execution a few nights later wasn't perfect, it was good enough, and we escaped with a 69-65 win, our first championship of the season.

The Pepsi Blue and Gold Classic matched us up with Sam Houston State in the opening round of the four-team tournament. I can see why Coach Crean was worried because, believe it or not, players know when they are "expected" to win. Early season games against less than formidable opponents help fund these opponents' athletic programs. In fact, most major Division 1 programs "buy" early season wins to help build their NCAA tournament resumes. It also prevents top teams from wearing down given the brutal schedules in today's power conferences. Money aside, we had to play the game, and the 84-71 victory secured us a spot in Saturday's championship game with Kent State.

Kent State has a strong basketball tradition and has made several appearances in the NCAA tournament. NFL great Antonio Gates was a basketball star there, and I still remember picking Kent in my NCAA tournament brackets as a kid. Every guy on the Kent State squad must've been instructed to try and intimidate us. Before the game, both teams were huddled inside the tunnel, anxious to take the floor. Trash talking is commonplace in the tunnel, so it wasn't surprising to see guys getting into it. This time, however, was different. One of the Kent State players was wearing a silver linked chain around his neck and was constantly barking like a dog. It was quite comical, especially since this guy sat on the bench with the chain on for the duration of the game. This wasn't a piece of jewelry, but a heavy chain, with thick links. Was he in the doghouse? Was he even on the team? I guess it didn't really matter. He barked, but we had the last bite, winning a tough game 66-61, with Travis collecting tournament MVP honors following a 14-point, 10-assist performance.

Two tournaments, two championships. I showed up to class on Monday wearing my triple XL BCA tournament champions t-shirt, which looked more like a dress. Mr. Dole, my accounting professor and the king of dry humor, looked me up and down, smiled, and said in a monotone voice, "Nice shirt."

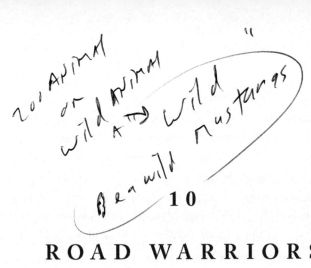

## 10

# ROAD WARRIORS

The following week would bring our first road game at Oakland University in Michigan. Playing on the road is tough at any level. When you've played in thousands of games and raucous environments, you'd think you'd almost be desensitized to what's going on in the stands. However, as a human being, I have to admit that I still see the fans waving noisemakers behind the basket. My ears aren't immune to the vulgar blasts that come from the student section, although I rarely listen to them. During my year at Minnesota Crookston, I'll never forget seeing a coach pay a group of eight guys following a game in which we were harassed from horn to horn. When fans know the names of your family members, it's hard not to pay attention. Obviously intoxicated, these guys were rewarded with a little more from where that came from. Winning on the road requires a focus that is often under-appreciated. Marquette actually had t-shirts made that week that said: "Wanted: Road Warriors." It was a subtle reminder of the type of mindset that would be required outside of the friendly confines of our home court.

To prepare for this game, we didn't do anything out of the ordinary. In fact, we continued the brutal practices that made Marquette famous during Crean's tenure. Crean knew that tough teams would win in tough environments, and he went the extra mile to ensure that we were tough. A subsequent t-shirt would read "Toughness is a Talent," and only the guys on the team truly understood what that meant. Crean being a Michigan native also added fuel to the fire, as everyone wants to win when they're "home." Unfortunately, because I had transferred from a scholarship school to another scholarship school, I was ineligible to travel with the team, even though I wasn't on scholarship at Marquette. Traveling with the team would've been a blast, as Marquette flew charter, stayed in nice hotels, and played teams from all over the country. My consolation (or punishment) for transferring was additional strength sessions with Scott. Fortunately, Dan Fitzgerald and Chris Teff were both in the same situation, so we had a three-man group. Dan had transferred from Tulane, and Chris ironically had played at Minnesota Crookston with me. Most of the road games were on television, so we would get together to watch the games. If the games weren't on television or the internet, we would follow the sports tracker on espn.com.

We handled Oakland on the road, 95-87, with our point total being the most we would score all year. This game, along with the next two vs. Delaware State and South Dakota State were tough to prepare for as players. Everyone is always excited to play, especially early in the season, but the excitement around the office doesn't come close to preparations for say, Wisconsin, who we would play next.

Mike Kinsella was a seven-footer that had spent a year at Rice before transferring to Minneapolis Tech and then finally Marquette. I was excited about Mike's potential because he had a soft touch for a big guy; unfortunately, he broke his foot in the preseason and was still rehabbing for most of our non-conference schedule. Having a guy like Mike was a missing piece for us, especially against teams like Wisconsin that had legitimate centers. Mike would pedal a Schwinn Airdyne bicycle in the corner of the gym during practice. Actually, I should re-phrase that. Scott would be breathing down his neck as he did bike sprints: one after another after another. As much as Mike biked, he probably could've traded his basketball shorts for a pair of spandex and signed up for a local cycling race.

Scott loved bike sprints. I feel like every good leg workout always had a few of them mixed in. Like every other part of the Marquette program, these weren't just sprints, but all-out bursts against the clock. If any of us didn't make the required distance (0.4 miles) in under a minute, the entire group would go again. It's one thing to let yourself down, but I know from personal experience how awful it felt to make everyone go again. Similar to the VersaClimber, getting to 0.4 miles meant all-out effort. Even then, there would be days when you'd put your head down and go balls to the wall, only to look up and see 0.38 and think to yourself, *There's no way!* The key is that you can't let your mind go to a place of dejection, as Scott would immediately re-set the timer to one minute, and you and your teammates would need to be ready.

An interesting thing about working out with Scott was that the workouts for Dan, Chris, and I were different than the rest of the team's. They were intentionally much harder and geared to gain strength and weight because we couldn't play in the games. The rest of the team would lift lighter weights and do fewer repetitions during the season to maintain strength but not wear down. I, on the other hand, gained 14 pounds during the season and actually lowered my body fat into the 5% range. Looking back at pictures, I also had a huge neck! Scott's program, like it or not, worked, and my physical development during the season was a direct reflection of that.

One thing that stood out about Scott's program was a lot of manual partner exercises. By this, I mean that one guy would hold a wooden bar, while the other provided resistance doing exercises like biceps curls and triceps presses. The challenge here was that you had resistance during 100% of the exercise. Often, I'd get paired up with Ousmane Barro, our 6'10" freshman center. Lying on my back for the triceps press, I'd push with everything I had, as Ousmane would push the wooden bar back at my face. On several occassions,

I thought, *If he doesn't let up, I'm going to get my face smashed.*

Because of the added time with Scott, we got to know him a bit better on a personal level, although what he shared was questionable. One day, I asked him how his weekend was, and he told me a story about a guy showing up at his house, uninvited. Apparently, the guy rang his doorbell, and when Scott opened the door, the guy was holding a golf club, ready to take a swing at him. I stood there listening intently but also thinking, *Why in the world did a guy show up at your front door with a golf club?* Anyways, Scott continued by explaining that he wrestled the guy to the ground and used the golf club to pin the guy down. "You know what the strongest bone in your body is, Willkom?" he asked. Before I could respond, he answered for me and said, "It's your forehead." Scott told us that he then proceeded to headbutt the guy in the face using his forehead, while pinning him down with the golf club. After the guy was no longer a threat, Scott called the police and told them that someone had been trespassing on his property.

I stood there, unsure of how to respond. *Nice job? Was the guy alright?* There were so many questions that I wanted to ask, but I refrained. To this day, I've never gotten a better response to, "How was your weekend?"

Playing Division 1 basketball is a grind, but it also has several perks, and you get to meet some notable people. Before our first practice of the season, Crean had the assistant general manager of the New York Knicks and a representative from Nike come in to talk to us. The Nike rep talked about the honor of being a Nike ELITE school. Nike created an exclusive line for schools that had made the Final Four in the past five years, and we would be rewarded with exclusive Nike ELITE shoes and gear. We received custom sweat suits that were charcoal, with gold lettering, and had the word ELITE printed down the leg. At the time, the rep also promised custom blue and gold shoes, a perk that got everybody in the room fired up. Unfortunately, the shoes never showed up, but Mike Thibault did. Mike had been in and around the NBA and

CBA for years, before becoming the head coach of the WNBA's Connecticut Sun in 2003. While Thibault didn't interact much with the players, he was certainly a trusted colleague of Crean's, often dropping in to check out practice.

Richard "Dick" Strong was an important booster to the Marquette program and was the only other "outsider" to frequent practice. Mr. Strong's financial services company was well known in the Milwaukee area, but I always wondered how much a booster has to donate to get that type of access, especially given how tight Crean ran the Marquette program.

Another obvious advantage was being able to meet former Marquette players, such as Dwayne Wade, Terry Sanders, Robert Jackson, and Jim McIlvaine. These guys represented the best of Marquette, with Dwayne, Terry, and Robert competing in the 2003 Final Four, and Jim having a nice NBA career. One guy that used to hang out around the gym was Milwaukee Brewers pitcher Ben Sheets. Sheets was great. He always wanted to play HORSE, and he would get after you with his Louisiana accent. I don't think I ever lost to Ben in HORSE, but then again, I never had the opportunity to challenge him in a baseball related activity. Sheets had a big upper body and loved to compete, which is why, despite his lack of basketball ability, he always wanted to play. I watched Sheets pitch several times when I was in college, and it was neat to have that connection to a professional athlete.

A final perk of playing basketball for Marquette is that you never went thirsty. The men's basketball locker room, which had a key code on the door, had a Gatorade machine in it. Unlike other Gatorade machines, this one was free, and the machine would allow you to take up to three twenty-ounce bottles at a time. The Gatorade machine came in handy in particular when the NCAA stopped by for random drug tests. Old men would show up and ask a random number of players to provide a urine sample. If you were selected, you had to provide a sample, regardless if you just left the urinal. Guys would routinely chug a couple Gatorades to expedite the process, which is interesting knowing that all that fluid probably compromised the accuracy of the sample.

On a similar note, Gatorade also provided nutritional shakes for post workout nutrition. The shakes came in chocolate, vanilla, and strawberry cans. One thing that I'm proud of is that Scott never supported or condoned supplements in the weight room. He was going to develop athletes naturally, and the only supplements we took were those Gatorade shakes. To gain fourteen pounds in a season while decreasing my body fat is remarkable given that fact. Looking back, my results probably would've been even more dramatic if nutrition would've been a bigger priority. Because I wasn't on scholarship, I ate dormitory food, buffet style, like every other college kid. In fact, a few of the cooks at the Schroeder Hall cafeteria used to make fun of me because I'd often show up for dinner with bags of ice wrapped around my knees or ankles. Eating aside, my physical transformation was 100% about the hard work I put in, and this will always remain the most tried and true way to transform your body.

Taking care of your body is essential at the college level. Practices are long and grueling, and you learn the importance of the training room early on. Jayd Grossman was our team trainer. Jayd had worked for Bob Huggins at Cincinnati, so he was used to the aftermath of tough, physical practices. In fact, it's hard to argue that any team was tougher than the Bearcats' 1999-2000 team that finished 29-4, led by Kenyon Martin, Pete Mickeal, DerMarr Johnson, and Steve Logan. Imagine being a fly in that gym! Jayd required every guy to wear ankle braces, unless they preferred to get taped every day. The philosophy was all about prevention. When I balked at one point about the braces slowing me down, I got a mean look, and that was the end of the conversation. For most of the season, I would practice with a football pad taped to my thigh to protect my quad after getting kneed early in the season. In today's game, players wear padded shorts, an invention that should have been mine had I possessed any foresight at all.

Another essential part of taking care of your body was utilizing the cold tub after practices. This wasn't your grandfather's old, silver tub full of ice like you see in the movies. Built like a hot tub into the ground, only with jets streaming ice cold water, the cold tub did wonders in relieving sore limbs, bruises, or strains. It hurt like hell to initially step into that water, but I'd start with my feet, then my knees, and eventually try to sit in there with the water to my shoulders, teeth chattering away. I am proud to say that I never missed a practice, despite days when I probably should've been on the sidelines. As harsh as this sounds, I was an expendable guy for Coach Crean. If I was lost for the season with an injury, life would go on, and Marquette would continue to win games. I understand the business of big-time college basketball, and coaches get paid to win games, no matter the cost. I'm not Coach Crean, nor can I read his mind, but there were times when I questioned whether Crean truly cared about the well-being of his players. In the last few years of Crean's tenure at Marquette, several notable players suffered season-ending injuries, such as Travis Diener, Dominic James, and Jerel McNeal. Pushing guys in practice is necessary, and I understand why a consistent dose of tough practices sets the right tone for a team. However, there's also a strategy to protecting your assets. I'm sure even Crean was second guessing himself when notable guys would crumble to the floor. There were days when practice was over, and like a lion awaiting his prey, Scott would be chomping at the bit to put us through extra work. Often, demanding practices would end, but before we could leave the gym, somehow, we'd be led back to the baseline to do wall sits.

Steve Novak, our 6'10" sharpshooter, used to joke about the difference between a program like Marquette and a program like Syracuse. At Marquette, practices were long and grueling from October to March. At Syracuse, Jim Boeheim preferred to shorten his practices as the season wore on, and they would rarely practice for more than ninety minutes come February. Novak liked a lot of things about Marquette, but I don't think he would've complained one bit had Crean adopted Boeheim's strategy.

Coach Crean actually ended a spirited practice early one day, and he praised all of us for our effort and focus. As Crean broke the huddle, I thought, *Is this really happening?* I walked out of the practice gym with Dameon Mason, and while I was feeling like a rockstar, he looked at me laughing, "Crean's going recruiting man!" Effort, focus, it could have been anything that day because Coach Crean had a plane to catch!

Before I could even make it to the locker room, Scott herded us all back to the weight room, where we would each have to do fifty leg presses before we were done for the day. There were two machines, and we were broken up into groups. While I had been through this leg press rodeo before, I stood there anxious, as I watched Scott load the machines up with weight, and more weight, and finally, another forty-five-pound plate on each side. I thought back to my first strength session with Scott, but immediately told myself that I couldn't go there. This was a new day, a new challenge. I watched Chris Teff and Chris Grimm both get to forty, and then fight for forty-five, and then agonize over those last five reps. Both those guys had me by at least fifty pounds, but I was up next and locked in. I made it to thirty, and like déjà vu, my legs started to shake. I stopped thinking about fifty and just focused on one: one breath, one push, one breath, one push. At forty-three, guys gathered around and started to cheer me on. "Come on Willkom, you got this." I made it to fifty, and as I crouched down to the floor to catch my breath, every guy on the team gave me a pat on the back. It's amazing what a difference being surrounded by a team can make. On day one, I was alone, and twenty reps was Mount Everest. Now, granted with less weight, I ripped off fifty reps, and I could've done more.

As I walked back to the locker room, Todd Townsend, one of our senior leaders, walked alongside. "Ya know, my first year here was so hard because you never knew if you were going to make it. But, once you prove to yourself that you can do it, you can do anything man." Todd was so right. To think about what he had been through in four years, you could've thrown anything in front of Todd, and he would have attacked it without a thought of failure.

# 11

# ASSISTANT COACHES

Assistant Coach Bo Ellis was the type of guy that everyone enjoyed being around. Bo's legacy on the Marquette campus goes back to his days as player in the 1970's. A three-time All-American, his 1977 national championship team was the greatest team in the history of Marquette basketball and is the standard to which all teams strive.

I met Bo during the summer of 2004 while working Marquette basketball camps. I was familiar with Bo's past, and I was most impressed by his appearance in the movie "Hoop Dreams," which is one of my all-time favorites. Bo had grown up in Chicago and starred at Parker High School before arriving at Marquette as a player. Following the '77 title run, Bo was picked 17th in the NBA draft and would play three seasons with the Denver Nuggets. He was later recognized for his creativity as well, as he was the mastermind behind the famous "untucked" jerseys that were eventually banned by the NCAA.

Every once in a while, a camper would approach Bo and ask him about his past. To most kids, though, he was just another coach on the staff that would yell at you if you were screwing around. While Bo flew under the radar of the kids, he certainly was in the limelight when parents showed up to camp. To many of them, Bo Ellis was a celebrity: a guy that they grew up admiring and imitating in their driveways. To his credit, Bo handled every picture request with a smile, and his relaxed demeanor was refreshing considering the adversity he had been through as a player, father, and coach. To clarify, Bo lost his 24-year-old daughter, Nikki, the previous summer to complications from an enlarged liver. Prior to Marquette, he had been the head coach at Chicago State, where he had a 23-104 record in four and a half seasons.

At the end of each week of camp, the camp coaches would have a party at a local bar or restaurant. Mo's Irish Pub was a popular destination, and Marquette paid the bill in appreciation for each coach's week of work. It was certainly a nice gesture from the Marquette staff, and coaches would return each summer because they appreciated the extra touch. Following a few drinks at Mo's, Bo and a few of the camp coaches decided to continue the party at Have a Nice Day Café on Milwaukee's Old World Third Street. There must have been five hundred people there, and I'm willing to bet that Bo knew every single one of them. Showing up to a bar with Bo made me feel important, and just as it's a privilege to accompany someone with fame or fortune, it was even more of an honor because Bo treated every one of us with respect and wanted to make sure we were having a good time.

Of course, my relationship with Coach Ellis was different once I joined the team. Bo worked primarily with our post players and helped facilitate the strong recruiting ties that Marquette had to the Chicago area. Despite my limited interaction with Coach Ellis, I'll never forget riding with him in his Chevy Trailblazer to one of our games. All the assistants drove a Trailblazer, while Crean sported a white Escalade. Pregame preparation at Marquette always consisted of student managers picking us up in university vans and transporting us to the game. However, due to a shortage of vans, the managers could only take eight guys in the van. Rather than make multiple trips, the assistant coaches volunteered to drive the rest of us to the game. It was a pregame ritual to crank Lil John in the van on the way to the Bradley Center, but Coach Ellis had a different idea. "You fellas need to appreciate some smooth jazz," he said. I remember sitting in that SUV thinking to myself, *If I had to guess what type of music Coach Ellis listened to, this would be it.* Bo was in the zone, the guys appreciated something new, and we won the game.

Coach Ellis was a major proponent of rebounding and boxing out. During box out drills, Crean would go ballistic at guys to get physical, reminding us more than once to "hit the mother fucker!" Bo, meanwhile, would say calmly, "You need to put the wood on em fellas."

One of Coach Ellis' trademarks was the hand pound, which he used to greet players and affirm a job well done. Bo had arthritis in his hands, and his knuckles were extremely hard and bony. He also wore his 1977 NCAA Championship ring. Getting a fist pound from Bo was like getting hit with a rock: it hurt like hell. Bo wasn't "hand tapping," he was "hand pounding," and I still smile about the thought of guys walking around shaking their hand following an exchange with Bo.

Coach Jason Rabedeaux, or Coach Rab, was the consummate jokester, a guy who had developed a reputation as a recruiter, most notably with Kelvin Sampson at Oklahoma. When Rab wasn't on his Bluetooth, he was keeping it real with the guys, willing to talk about anything. In fact, Rab's greatest asset, his personality, was an outstanding complement to Crean's hard-nosed, business-like demeanor. Although I never spent a great deal of time with Rab one-on-one, it was comforting to know that there was a guy like that on the staff. During practice, Rab's main role was to get us warmed up, and his drill of choice consisted of curling layups, followed by short jumpers. Apparently, Rab could shoot the basketball back in the day, although his only shots at Marquette were usually verbally directed at the underclassmen. Rab also rotated with Jeff Strohm in preparing game plans for our next opponent. The game plan always consisted of a typed scouting report, video clips, and on-court demonstrations and drills to prepare us for what we were going to see.

From the start of the season, Rab made it a point to join us in the weight room. He wasn't there to lift weights, but he sure would break a sweat. Presumably trying to shed a few pounds, Rab would work out on the stair stepper or treadmill like a mad man. At the end of each workout, Rab looked like he had just jumped into a swimming pool! It didn't take long for the guys to poke fun at Rab, calling him "Fat Rab" and making other snide remarks regarding his weight. Rab had that gift of give and take, and to his credit, being the brunt of the joke allowed him to develop the relationship between coach and player that every coach strives for.

Following a few seasons at Marquette, Rab actually went overseas to coach a team in China and later Vietnam. He blogged about his team on occasion, and several of the posts were featured on Marquette's website. In 2015, Jason Rabedeaux passed away in Saigon, Vietnam, following off-and-on battles with alcohol. He was 49. Wright Thompson, of ESPN, wrote a detailed feature story about his life, and I encourage everyone to check it out. The game certainly misses Rab, and there wasn't anybody quite like him.

Jeff Strohm was our third assistant and had joined the staff in the spring of 2002, after five years with Rick Majerus at the University of Utah. If Bo was cool and calm and Rab the life of the party, Strohm was the all business, "let's do everything perfect" kind of guy. It made sense, as that had always been Majerus's style as well. Strohm was tough; I'd run a play with the scout team seemingly just the way he wanted. "You 'gotta cut harder!" he'd yell. "Do it again!" Every practice, his shirt would be soaked with sweat; an impressive feat, given his lean frame. And yet, his hair was always perfectly combed to the side. Whatever hair gel he was using obviously worked.

Bo, Rab, and Strohm were all talented in different ways, but this was ultimately Crean's team. A moment I'll never forget occurred at halftime of one of our games. I don't remember the opponent, but we had struggled in the first half and were seated in the locker room of the Bradley Center waiting for Coach Crean. Because of my transfer situation, I wasn't allowed by NCAA rules to suit up for the games, so I was in dress clothes. As we waited for Coach, guys uttered the usual "Let's go," and "Pick it up." Crean entered the locker room in a rage, with a look on his face that made it tough to look him in the eye. After several expletives about our play, he said, "Willkom, stand up." At that point, I thought, *Why in the world would he call me out?* I hadn't played a second, and I was wearing a peach colored dress shirt and the only dress shoes I owned. Motive aside, I stood up, and I could tell that several of my teammates were probably thinking the same thing. "You have been bullshittin all week!" he barked, still displaying that anger in his eyes. After a few more choice words, he went on to explain that I was the reason that our guys were playing so poorly, because I had done such a poor job preparing them for the game. "Now, sit down!" he yelled. Crean stormed out of the locker room and left a silent group of men, heads down, thinking about what he had said.

After a minute or two, Dameon Mason began to chuckle. Then Travis joined in, and they couldn't believe that Crean had called me out. In fact, they both joked that if they had any more bad games, they wouldn't have to worry because I'd be the one getting blamed. From Crean's perspective, though, I think he wanted everyone to know that every guy on our team mattered. Practices were my games, and if I performed poorly, I certainly wasn't doing my job of getting my teammates ready to play in the actual games. I don't remember practicing poorly, but the point wasn't how I practiced. Rather, it was understanding that my contribution counted and was valued. At the time, I was upset for being called out. Years later, I appreciate the fact that Crean respected and valued my contribution and made me accountable like everyone else.

# 1 2

# WISCONSIN WEEK

Wisconsin vs. Marquette. For those of us born in the state of Wisconsin, this was the game that was circled every year in August when the schedule was released. To add fuel to the fire, my former AAU teammate, Brian Butch, was a key cog for the Badgers, along with Alando Tucker. Preparing for Wisconsin was different than our other games, as guys like Steve and Travis made sure that everyone stayed focused for that entire week leading up to the game. A loss to Wisconsin wouldn't make or break our season, but pride is a powerful tool, especially when your two superstars are Wisconsin natives. Rumor has it that Wisconsin wanted both Travis and Devin Harris coming out of high school. However, Harris told Wisconsin that he would go somewhere else if they signed Travis.

Anyway, three days before the game, several of us were running the swing offense to prepare the starters for the motion they would see from the Badgers. Halfway through the workout, Dameon Mason slipped through one of my screens, and Coach Crean went absolutely nuts. "How can you grow up in Wisconsin and not know how to set a screen?" he shouted! I knew how to set a screen, but I had no idea what I was doing wrong. Crean wanted me to get extremely physical with guys, to set illegal screens, and challenge guys to fight through them. I was essentially tasked with being an offensive lineman for the week and was asked to do whatever it took to keep guys from getting through.

It wasn't the first time that we were asked to do things that weren't allowed. Box out drills at Marquette were essentially void of any rules at all. The mission: get the ball at all costs. Guys would push, claw, elbow, knee: anything to get position. Depending on Crean's mood, if a shot went up and the defense didn't get the rebound, we'd often run for every missed opportunity. Jerseys were torn, blood shed, and everything in between. I took an elbow to the side of the head one day, and I stood there a bit delirious. "Hey, are you ok?" asked Steve Novak. Before I could respond, he said, "You need to go to the locker room." Blood poured down the side of my face, and I would need several stiches near my right ear.

Marquette fans would see our team commit fouls in games that were a direct reflection of things allowed in practice not being allowed in a game. It's hard to know whether we gained an advantage or not, but the sheer effort to withstand those drills made them a net positive in my mind.

Drills like this also came to define the Marquette brand of basketball. Dating all the way back to the 1970's when Al McGuire said, "If you haven't broken your nose in basketball, you haven't really played. You've just tokened it" (Kertscher). This wasn't a place where you went to play finesse basketball.

We went on to beat Wisconsin in front of a sold-out crowd on our home floor. Although the win surprised a lot of folks in the media, I certainly wasn't surprised. The one thing that did surprise me, however, was the defense Chris Grimm played on Alando Tucker. Part of Crean's game plan was to have the 6'10" Grimm defend the 6'5" Tucker, with everyone else playing gap defense to prevent Tucker from getting into the lane. Often underappreciated, Chris Grimm was an excellent defender with great feet for a guy his size. In all my years of basketball, I had never seen a player defend a screen and roll with the type of effort and intensity that Grimm brought to the table. In fact, with the amount of pick and roll basketball that we played at Marquette, Grimm was an expert at "blitzing" screens. Rather than "show," which is how most post defenders play a screen and roll, Grimm would often "blitz" the ball handler by steering him vertically towards half court. Those familiar with the game know how difficult it is for any post defender to contain a ball handler that is trying to turn the corner. I knew firsthand how good Grimm was because at 6'0", it's not easy to see when you have two defenders essentially doubling you off the screen and roll.

Grimm's effort that day defending Tucker was sensational, as he kept him out of the middle of the floor all game. While Tucker was a big-time player, his outside shot was flat and inconsistent, and we would give him perimeter jump shots all game.

Midway through the second half, Travis Diener drove the lane and was fouled hard by Badgers center Brian Butch. If you recall, I had played on the same AAU team as Butch in high school, and we were friends. What ensued got me more television time than I would get the rest of my life. As Diener tried to get up, Butch bumped him, and the two started jawing at each other. Some of the other players were getting involved, and whistles were blowing, with the officials trying to regain control of the game. Now, a TV timeout was scheduled to take place, and with the whistles blowing, I assumed the timeout had been called. Chris Teff and I ran out on the floor like every other time out, and I went and grabbed Travis to pull him back to our huddle. I yelled something at Butch, and Travis, Chris, and I headed back towards our bench. Bo Ryan, Wisconsin's head coach, started arguing with the officials that 1. Travis should receive a technical foul and 2. Marquette players left the bench and should also receive a technical. The officials went to half court and brought both coaches together. There were no monitors for the officials to review at the time. Meanwhile, the sold-out crowd of 18,000+ in the Bradley Center was going crazy, and everyone was on their feet. While the officials' conversation lasted a mere thirty seconds, Crean and Ryan continued to scream at each other in a heated exchange. "That's bull shit!" Ryan yelled, and Crean fired back, "Fuck you!" When the officials announced that no technical fouls had been assessed and Travis would go to the line for two shots, the Marquette game producers immediately queued "Thunderstruck" by ACDC, and it was the loudest I had experienced at the Bradley Center. You couldn't have scripted better drama to add to an in-state rivalry that already was a little salty. After the game, Crean congratulated everyone on the victory and then said to Chris Teff and I, "Don't you ever think about leaving the bench again, or I will kick you off the team."

After the game, students, fans, and friends told me that I had been on TV pulling Travis away from Butch. I wouldn't say I was proud of that moment, but I think it solidified the family bond that many teams claim to have but don't. I had my teammate's back, and he would have had mine. Butch and I would later laugh about it. After the game, I got a lot of flak in the dorms about leaving the bench and putting myself in the middle of a scuffle. It is funny how moments like that are retold by the people that witnessed what happened, as different angles from the stands seemed to produce different stories.

# 1 3

# CHRISTMAS BREAK

A week before Christmas, we had a highly anticipated matchup with Arizona at the Bradley Center. Arizona week was a blast for me because I was instructed to be Salim Stoudamire for the next five days. After watching him on film, there were three things that I had to do in practice every day: drive left, be selfish, and shoot a lot. Stoudamire was a talented scorer, a lefty, and had unlimited range for an undersized two guard. He also had a bad attitude, and media reports during the week wavered as to whether Lute Olson would even have him suit up. Regardless, we prepared with him in the lineup, and I took a lot of NBA threes that week.

Saturday rolled around, and game time was scheduled for 12:00 noon. For the basketball fan, this was great, but we hated it as players. Arizona agreed to a 7:00 a.m. shoot around, and we were scheduled to take the floor at eight. As practice approached (a Marquette shoot around was always referred to as a practice because we rarely did any shooting), I was sitting on a folding chair, tying my shoes, and waiting for Arizona to leave the court. As guys made their way off the floor, Lute Olson walked over, shook my hand, said good morning, and then said, "Ya know, this is way too darn early for me!" I laughed, and we chatted about how nice the Arizona weather would be later that day on December 18. Lute Olson had a charisma about him, a likeability, and I could tell in five minutes from watching him with his team that his players respected him. Years later, I would read Olson's book, *The Seasons of My Life*, and have an even deeper respect for his journey to the top of the coaching echelon. We played well that day but ultimately lost to a better team. Guys like Stoudamire, Channing Frye, and Mustafa Shakur would go on to play in the NBA, and that Lute Olson guy kind of knew what he was doing.

One of the toughest parts about playing college basketball is essentially giving up your entire Christmas break. Most college students have about a month around Christmas to go home, spend time with their friends and families, and refresh their minds and bodies following finals week. At Marquette, we had Christmas Eve and Christmas day off, returning for a mid-afternoon practice on December 26. Because I didn't have a car, my mother drove me from Marshfield down to Milwaukee and teared up as she said goodbye. As tough as I had been programmed to become, it was extremely hard for me to say goodbye to my mom. I felt like I was being robbed of time with the people that mattered most to me.

Even deeper, I was reminded of the previous year when I was home for two days from Minnesota Crookston. Going back to Crookston was one of the hardest things I've ever done. I absolutely loved being home, eating home-cooked meals, and having snowball fights with my siblings. The winterim period in Crookston was absolutely dead: there wasn't a soul on campus, the dorm was empty, and even the cafeteria was closed. Adam Sullivan, Matt Draxten, and I were the only three people in the dorm. We were given a per diem of $30/day for food, and being the businessmen that we were, we spent most of our money buying groceries and cooking gourmet meals in the dormitory kitchen. We rented movies, played video games, and talked about life. We even ventured over to a nearby Super 8 motel, where we'd sneak in the back door and sit in the hot tub. For a two-week period in sub-zero temperatures, this was all we did, along with daily practice. To say we were socially deprived was an understatement. To make matters worse, Matt Draxten invited us to a New Year's Eve party at his friend's cabin. I drove Adam's car, and it was such a great feeling just to get out of the dorm. After the party, we drove back to Crookston and tried to mentally prepare for an 8:00 a.m. practice on New Year's Day. The ensuing practice was horrific, a bloodbath of sprints, and luckily, I wasn't hurting as bad as most of the guys. I'll never forget the absolute tongue lashing that we received from head coach Jeff Oseth. As bad as it was, I only remember Oseth yelling, "You guys are out fuckin' around, sippin' beers, and chasing pussy." And then we were back on the line for another sprint.

Marquette's winterim period was a time to work, period. Coach Crean took advantage of NCAA rules and us being out of school and held two-a-day practices. Every day, we would get up early and practice from about 8:00 to 10:00 a.m., working exclusively on individual skill development. The drills were similar to what we did in individual workouts in the offseason, and for some reason, we did a lot of Mikan drills. For those not familiar, the Mikan drill consists of layups back and forth, both facing the basket and in reverse. The afternoon session was run more like a regular practice, with a lot of focus on new offensive sets. If Crean had a strength as a basketball coach, he certainly knew offense and had hundreds of plays. On a negative note, because we had so many sets, guys would often make mistakes, and younger guys, in particular, had a hard time remembering them all. Our two freshmen big men, Ryan Amoroso and Ousmane Barro, were earning additional minutes, but their inability to execute impromptu play calls often limited their actual game time.

Ousmane and Ryan were also pushed extremely hard by Travis. Here were two guys that couldn't have been more different. Ouse was from Senegal, by way of Chicago, and was really quiet, slight in build, and very much learning the game. "Amo," on the other hand, hailed from Burnsville, MN, was loud and animated, and was much more physically developed. Travis would go as far as to throw basketballs at these guys from close range to get them to catch the ball. I'm not talking Mike Rice Jr. style, the former Rutgers coach, who was fired for throwing basketballs at players, but more, *You better learn to catch the ball, otherwise I'm never going to pass it to you.* Travis would let both guys know when he wasn't happy, and it wasn't pretty. As harsh as it often came across, this all stemmed from the most intense desire for Travis to win. When Ouse got beat out for a 50/50 ball during a game in January, Travis almost maniacally exploded, "Just get the fucking ball!" Similar to how I talked about fear either paralyzing or motivating you, as the season progressed, both Ryan and Ousmane started to toughen up. It was a process that had to happen, and Travis was the catalyst. For fans that talk about senior leadership, this was it, happening right in front of me, and yet not the way that leadership is often envisioned.

One thing that Scott was a stickler about was weighing in before every strength & conditioning session. For guys like me, it didn't seem to matter as much, but for young post players who were trying to gain weight, it was imperative that these guys ate outside of team meals. Ousmane showed up to the weight room after a weekend off and had lost a few pounds. In a move that was half crazy and half to prove a point, Scott had him drink Gatorade protein shakes until he couldn't drink any more. If there was a "psycho line," Scott constantly straddled it.

Because the Haggerty House where I lived was closed for break, I lived with video coordinator Luke Benish for a few weeks in Humphrey Hall. Although he was still a "coach," I appreciated Luke's ability to have a personality outside of basketball. Of all the guys on the staff, I could talk openly and honestly about practice, school, life, whatever, and I didn't have to worry about getting scolded for my opinions. Luke knew how tough it was, and he lived it, just from a different angle. If Crean needed film on a team, requests were often made at 11:00 p.m., and Luke would make sure it was done before Crean arrived back at the office the next morning. Like Luke, Andy Klister, our team manager, would go out of his way for Marquette basketball. Andy got paid, but when you calculate his dollars earned per hour, he made minimum wage look like winning the lottery.

Humphrey Hall was where the scholarship players lived, and the apartments were nice compared to the dorms, but the building was still relatively old. To put things in perspective, I hung out in Kris Humphries apartment the year before at the University of Minnesota, and that place was BALLIN! Like the winter period in Crookston, Marquette's campus didn't have much going on. However, the city of Milwaukee is a bit livelier than the rural Crookston. It was also nice that all the scholarship players were living at Humphrey. At most schools, upperclassmen can live wherever they want, which limits team bonding off the court. Coach Oseth at Crookston had told me that no matter where I went to college, I would face the same challenges over winter break. No disrespect, but that simply wasn't true. In Milwaukee, people were out and about, I was busy with basketball, and I had friends in Humphrey to hang out with. There were also restaurants within walking distance, and although my cooking skills were top notch by that point, we spent a lot of time at Cousins Subs and China Garden's all you can eat buffet.

During the winter break, we also got another player, Niv Berkowitz, who Strohm had recruited from Israel. Niv was a 6'3" guard, with wavy hair, and a herky-jerky style of play. Because Brandon Bell had been dismissed from the team prior to the season, Travis was our only true point guard with any experience. I was ineligible to play due to transfer rules, and Rob Hanley, a fellow walk-on, was a freshman.

Niv and Ryan Amoroso had a special connection, and to Ryan's credit, he did a great job making him feel welcome. Niv spoke limited English, but after only two practices, he was thrown into action and scored his first point on a free throw against Nebraska. Niv was used to a different style of play in Israel, and after practices, his comments always seemed to center on the amount of running, the time we spent in the weight room, and the physicality that was allowed in practice.

In mid-February, after only seven games, Niv was homesick and returned to Israel. I really liked Niv, but he was a bit of a fish out of water, and I'm sure his introduction to Scott in the weight room was similar to the rest of ours.

After one of our morning practice sessions, we gathered at center court as usual, only this time Crean said, "John Willkom, stand up." Now if you remember the last time he said this, it certainly didn't turn out in my favor, so I slowly made my way up from the floor. "We got first semester grades," he said. "Oh shit," said one of the guys, triggering a chuckle from the rest of the team. "Seriously though," Crean remarked. "Johnny Willkom with a 3.9 GPA…. that a boy!" he exclaimed. Everybody clapped, and Crean joked that he knew there was a reason I was on the team. "I'm just teasing you," he said. "Keep up the good work."

As I left the gym that day, I was so proud of where I was. Having spent a year in Crookston, Minnesota, I had experienced the isolation of being far from home at a small school. For nine months, I had persevered through unhappiness, kept my grades up, and maintained a vision for my life. Most importantly, I knew there was something better out there for me, and I kept the faith that something would turn out. Transferring schools caused me to lose sixteen academic credits, a full semester at most schools, and I had to take eighteen credits that fall to get back on track. All the other guys on the team were taking twelve credits, which meant I was taking two more classes. I may have had every reason to make excuses, but this, of all things, was toughness personified.

*Wisconsin state champion in the 400-meter dash (1994).*

*Handling the ball for Joe's All Stars.*

*With mentor and friend, Joe Konieczny, for my confirmation.*

*Fox Valley Skillz 9th Grade AAU Team (2000). I wore #33. My best friend, Luke Knauf, is #55. Future Wisconsin Badgers center, Brian Butch, is #42.*

*Shaking hands with high school coach, Gordie Sisson, after signing my scholarship to play basketball at Minnesota Crookston. My middle school basketball coach, Joe Konieczny, came to show his support.*

*Driving the ball for Minnesota Crookston vs. Bemidji State.*

*Being introduced at a Marquette scrimmage.*

*Signing autographs with Marquette teammate, Chris Teff.*

*Coach Cooks and I at Marquette's Midnight Madness.*

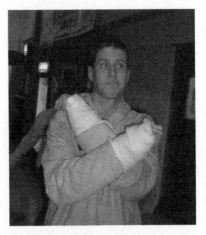

*Despite two broken wrists, I managed to return to coaching and graduate on time.*

*Matt Terry and I with our 3rd grade basketball team in Salt Lake City.*

*Salt Lake City East High School freshman team after winning 3rd place in the city tournament. Coaches Gianni Ellefson and Terrence Lord were instrumental to our success.*

*Kevin Albers and I meeting Aaron Rodgers in Park City, UT.*

*Chicago's Old St. Mary's 4th grade boys' basketball team.*

*When you love the game, you find ways to play it (even with a little snow on the ground).*

# 1 4

# F I L M

Coach Crean had a philosophy called "Maximize the Day," which challenged all of us in the offseason to do something extra every day to make us a better basketball player. A chart was posted in the locker room for players to write down their activities. Examples included shooting a hundred extra three-pointers, studying film for an hour, or working on footwork and finishing moves. To some, it may seem like a minimal request. However, picture a day in September when you wake up at 5:30 a.m., have conditioning from 6:00-7:30, class from 8:00-12:00, lunch until 1:00, individual workouts from 1:30-2:30, 5 on 5 scrimmaging from 3:00-5:00, dinner from 5:00-6:00, and study hall from 6:00-8:00 p.m. Imagine walking back to the Al McGuire Center after a day like this, lacing up your shoes, getting loose, and working hard for another hour. Win or lose, this is how dedicated the players at Marquette are, and I certainly hope fans respect the sheer amount of work that goes into the final product.

One of my jobs as a walk-on was to study opponents' point guards and bring that style of play to practice in preparation for a game. There was one opponent, Memphis, that I was excited about because I got to be Darius Washington for the week. Washington was a heralded freshman, known for his offensive prowess and occasional bad shot selection. A year earlier, his high school team had played against Sebastian Telfair's on ESPN at a time when televising high school games was virtually unheard of. Assistant coach Brian Wardle had me wear a blue headband and Memphis jersey and instructed me to shoot whenever I touched the ball. In fact, Crean actually yelled at me for not shooting after driving the lane and dishing to a wide-open teammate for a dunk. "Washington wouldn't do that," he clamored. Our scout team was comprised of me, Coach Wardle, Chris Teff, Shane Grube, Rob Hanley, and a rotation of post players: Ousmane Barro, Ryan Amoroso, Chris Grimm, etc. Playing on the scout team was great because I wasn't on such a tight leash. Other scenarios similar to Darius Washington included instructions only to drive, shoot three-pointers, or handle the ball like I was on the playground. Whatever it was, I had fun playing this style of basketball and embraced the task of being the best mimic I could be. It also gave me an appreciation for my basketball I.Q. Being able to physically execute everything on the basketball floor and understanding what needs to be done are two different things. God didn't bless me with great height, a long wingspan, or incredible jumping ability, but I was always thankful that I understood what Crean was trying to do and appreciated the various strategies.

Coach Wardle was the star on our scout team. A do-it-all scorer during his days as a player at MU, he actually finished third on the all-time scoring list when he graduated. At 6'5", he could do a little bit of everything, making him a tough cover for anyone that attempted to guard him. In addition to his skills on the floor, Wardle was an absolutely fierce competitor. In fact, he often got into it with the players and would even run sprints with the rest of us if we lost a drill. If we needed a go-to basket, Wardle was our guy, and it was amazing how sharp his game was considering he hadn't "played" in two years.

Winning on the scout team was hard because Crean made it that way. We were the "Gold" team, while the starters played on the "Blue" squad. Like anything else, the more you play against an opponent, the better you know their strengths, weaknesses, etc.

Crean would take the Blue squad aside and dictate what he wanted run. Often, we knew what was coming, but any negative result always gave the ball back to the Blue team. Earlier in practice, I was getting blasted for not fouling guys hard enough, but then I'd let a guy shoot an open jump shot, and Crean would call a foul if he missed? It was "Busch League" at its finest. At the same time, we all learned to battle no matter what, and it almost prepared us for future life challenges when you know you're getting screwed, but you can't let that detract from the next play, negotiation, or business deal.

After practice one day, Wardle pulled me aside and said, "Let me see your fingernails." I almost started laughing because I bite my nails on a daily basis and didn't have much to show. "Travis has been getting scratched a lot lately, and we want to make sure it's not you." I showed Brian my nails while thinking to myself, *Maybe Travis has a pet cat in his apartment?*

Instances like this epitomized the paranoia that invaded our program. A few weeks into the season, I did an interview over the phone for the Marshfield News Herald, my hometown newspaper. They asked me about the practices and playing on the team, and I responded openly and honestly. The day after the Wisconsin game, the story ran on the front page of the Sports section, along with a recap of the game. The next morning before practice, Wardle and Crean confronted me on the practice floor and asked me about the story. I was proud of it, had nothing to hide, and explained that I talked to someone on the phone a few weeks before the story was printed. Little did I know that all media requests were to be funneled through the MU athletics department, and all interviews were to be conducted in their presence. Crean and Wardle obviously never thought that I would be interviewed in any circumstance, and therefore, didn't have me participate in the team's preseason media training session. I listened to them yell while thinking, *What did I do wrong?* Not a believer in canned interviews, I was forced to use: "I'm just doing everything I can to help the team win" moving forward.

Friends and family often asked me about game preparation. To most fans, watching a game is about being entertained and seeing their team come out on top. Now, granted I say most fans, because there are die-hard basketball fans out there that do watch the game differently and pay close attention to the details. For instance, people close to Marquette basketball would make comments like, "The team sure did a great job last night getting three stops in a row on defense." This was a statistic that was kept every game, and one that we, as players, took great pride in. Getting three stops, though, was as much about preparation as it was about effort. Watching film, simulating matchups in practice, and reviewing the opposition's offensive sets were standard weekly protocols. In fact, a few days before each game, we would get a scouting report with information on the opposition's players and sets. The reports were long and very detailed, and Coach Rab and Coach Strohm would take turns putting them together. Whoever put the report together would also run us through these sets in practice. For instance, if St. Louis ran a certain play when the shot clock was getting low, we would have reviewed the set multiple times in practice before we would ever see it in a game. It was extremely gratifying for me (and I'm sure the coaching staff) to see guys make plays as a result of the scouting report.

Watching film was something that we did in Crookston during my freshman year, but Marquette took it to a whole new level. At Crookston, we would wheel out a 27" television on a stand and pop in a videotape of our opponent. At MU, we had a film room upstairs at the Al McGuire Center that featured a monster screen, projector, DVD player, and stadium seating. It was like watching a movie at your favorite theater. Crean's rules during film were to make eye contact with him when he talked and stay awake. Of course, staying awake in that "theater" wasn't easy when you were overtired and often physically exhausted following a workout/practice. Once the lights were dimmed, there were plenty of days when I could feel my head bobbing, and I literally fought to keep my eyes open. On the flip side, there were days when coaches would rip into you, and as much as I wanted to bury my head, I'd maintain eye contact, listen to their feedback, and do my best to apply it.

Following our second preseason scrimmage, Coach Rab was running through some clips and pointed out a shot I had missed from the left baseline with the shot clock about the expire. Dameon Mason had missed the rim badly on a jumper. I grabbed the rebound on the weak side, and with two seconds left on the shot clock, missed a short, ten-foot floater. Watching it again, it looked like a heads-up play to get a good shot off before the buzzer. True to the player/coach roles, Rab shouted out, "Willkom, what the hell was that?!" "Um, the shot clock was running down so I shot it so we…" "It's a shitty ass shot, that's what it is!" he yelled before I could finish my rationale. Travis looked at me and smiled, and Rab went on to break down (criticize) the rest of the scrimmage.

You learn early on that even if you're right, you never challenge a coach in front of the rest of the team. If Rab said I took a bad shot during our film study, then I took a bad shot. Every guy had plenty of days when they wanted to stand up and say, "You know what coach, you're wrong." However, and this is part of maturing as an adult, you bite your tongue and accept the feedback the best that you can. Granted, guys like Travis and fellow senior, Todd Townsend, could converse with the staff because there was a trust there, even if their viewpoints were exactly the same as one of the underclassmen's.

Apart from breaking down tape, Crean used the film sessions more to verbally motivate us than at any other time of our day. The talks could be energizing, or they could be extremely negative depending on the mood Crean was in. During one film session, Crean was explaining how a local television station had questioned the talent that Crean had recruited to Marquette. Crean proceeded to break down in tears, explaining the love and commitment that he had to every guy in the room that he had recruited. He talked about their families, and the psychologist in him wanted us to feel like the members of the media doubted us and our abilities. We'd heard the "us against the world" metaphor too many times. I didn't buy it for a minute, and neither did the guys in the room. As tough as Crean was, it just wasn't fathomable to see a guy like that spontaneously break down into tears. In fact, just fifteen minutes before that, he was absolutely blasting Ryan Amoroso for his box outs.

A few years later, Crean's recruitment of Chicago point guard Iman Shumpert was well-documented. On the first day that coaches could officially meet with recruits, Crean pulled up to Shumpert's house in a limousine at 12:01 a.m. dressed in a tuxedo. Crean obviously wanted to make an impression that he would go above and beyond to get Shumpert to Marquette. Shumpert didn't buy it and signed with Georgia Tech.

For me, this story epitomized Crean's personality as a coach. Everything in the media was always positive and upbeat. He had a unique charisma, energy, and almost physchotic drive to win. Yet, behind closed doors, Crean was rarely in a good mood and carried a smirk on his face to make sure everyone knew it. Crean could put on a front with the best of them by consistently keeping his players on edge, but the minute a reporter, recruit, or parent came into the picture, he could transform into a completely different person. I still don't think he's a bad guy, but you can only act like that for so long before your players' attitudes turn negative and become immune to that style of coaching.

Late-night film sessions usually involved food from Boston Market. I'm not sure why Boston Market, but the entire team loved it. I would order turkey, mashed potatoes, and everything else that came with it. Not being on scholarship meant taking advantage of meals like this, and it was always a treat to eat non-dormitory food.

Luke Benish was our video coordinator at Marquette. I met Luke during the summer of 2004 working MU basketball camps in June and July. He, like many of the players, understood that his job was a journey: a roller coaster ride that could hit the top or bottom at any moment. He had no set schedule, and requests would pour in at all hours of the day. Despite the chaos, Luke was great at what he did: he filmed every practice and game and was constantly editing tapes of opponents, players, etc. To Crean's credit, he would routinely request game tape of a player executing a teaching point that he wanted to emphasize. For example, he would have Luke put together clips of Jackson Vroman's (Iowa State) post game and show them to Chris Grimm. On a similar note, Travis would watch clips of Steve Nash reading the defense in pick and roll situations. Like I said earlier, I had watched film during my time in Crookston but had never experienced this level of thought and detail. While I'm sure it felt like a thankless job on many occasions, we were a better team because of Luke Benish.

# 15

# GAMES & MORE GAMES

Our season had been rock solid, and we were 13-1 going into a road contest at Memphis. Our only loss, the aforementioned 48-43 grinder to Arizona was to a formidable opponent, and we were right where we wanted to be heading into the teeth of our conference season. Memphis was no joke, boasting the likes of Rodney Carney, Sean Banks, Jeremy Hunt, and Darius Washington. They also had a freshman named Joey Dorsey that was built like an aircraft carrier and would go on to have a tremendous college career. Unlike our team, Memphis had played an extremely tough non-conference schedule. At 8-7, they certainly didn't look like a formidable foe on paper, but their losses included tough games against Syracuse, Pittsburgh, Texas, and Maryland. Although we played them tough, we just couldn't get over the hump, suffering a 78-68 setback. Fortunately for us, we got to come home to nurse our wounds and persevered two nights later, 66-64, in a thriller with South Florida. Todd Townsend had a huge dunk in that game that disproved my theory that four years of Scott Holsopple would decrease your vertical jump (just kidding, Scott).

The following week, we were headed to Rosemont, IL, to battle with the DePaul Blue Demons. Because the game was within driving distance from Milwaukee, Dan Fitzgerald, Chris Teff, and I piled into Dan's car and made our way across the border. While NCAA rules prohibited us from sitting on the bench, we were allowed to sit right behind it. Heading into the game, we were still ranked at #25 in the country, but this was a must win game for us given our lackluster play the previous week. Drake Diener, Travis's cousin and high school teammate from Fond du Lac, WI, starred for DePaul, along with Quemont Greer, a Milwaukee Vincent High School alum. While the focus all week had been on limiting Drake and Q's touches, it was Sammy Mejia, a 6'6" sophomore guard that lit us up for 26. Another sophomore, Lorenzo Thompson, who came into the game averaging three points per game, scored 17 in seventeen minutes! We could live with Sammy, but Lorenzo's outburst proved too much, and we fell 85-72, despite shooting 48% from the field.

Losses like this stung because they were typically followed by brutal practices. Nobody likes to lose, and we felt just as bad as the coaching staff. Walking back onto the practice floor, we warmed up with Coach Rab like usual. A few minutes later, Crean burst through the doors and lashed out in a "fuck-filled" tantrum. "On the line!" he barked. "22" after "22" proceeded. After running sprints for what seemed like a half hour, I kept thinking, *This has to be the last one*, but it wasn't. Guys were bent over at the waist, soaked in sweat. There was a basketball clock up on the wall that was re-set to twenty-two seconds immediately after we'd finish. I took a quick glance over to our student manager running the clock, who looked like he was going to cry as Crean told him to get the thing re-set faster. "Again!" Crean hollered. Crossing the baseline with one second remaining on the clock, followed by a loud buzzer, I wanted to fall over. I grabbed my knees, trying to get more air into my lungs. "On the line!" The whistle blew, and I took off again. Barely making it across the line, Crean informed us that someone hadn't finished in time. "Again, you mother fuckers!" he wailed. I was positioned next to Joe Chapman, and rather than look around, I focused on trying to stay slightly ahead of Joe. I don't remember how many sprints we ran that day. There were no water breaks, no time to think, no time to reflect on losing to DePaul.

I sat in the cafeteria that night, holding a piece of pizza and staring at the wall. It was almost as if I was half present, as it probably took me an hour to finish a single slice. I had been through enough of these that my natural response should've been, *Tomorrow will be better*. On that night, though, sometimes you just have to call a spade a spade. *That entire thing absolutely sucked.*

We had played three of our first four Conference USA games on the road, so guys were excited to return home to the Bradley Center to play Charlotte. Despite Ryan and Ousmane stepping up to the tune of 22 points, we fell 76-66, as Charlotte shot 10-21 from three to our 5-24.

Four nights later, we headed to Louisville to play the twelfth-ranked Cardinals, and we desperately needed a win to halt our two-game losing streak. Travis was hurt, and despite wanting to play, the coaches held him out. What ensued illustrated how valuable he was to our team. We got absolutely crushed, 99-52, and Larry O'Bannon went off for 30 points. It was Marquette's worst margin of defeat ever, breaking a mark that had stood since 1940. We also gave up seventeen three-pointers (six to O'Bannon), which was another MU record. When asked about Travis, Crean would say, "He means a lot to our club, and we learned how much tonight" (Rutherford). Games like this teach you a lot about yourself because despite the crazy margin of defeat, the loss would count the same as any other loss. Our ability to bounce back would challenge the very core of the Marquette program, and boy would we need it.

It's amazing what coaches will do to motivate their teams. Before our next game in St. Louis, Crean replayed a St. Louis television announcer's thoughts regarding our team. At one point, the guy said, "They've got nothing down low. They have nobody skilled enough to make those shots." He, of course, was referring to our lack of post play, which had been an Achilles' heel at Marquette for several years. After the film study, Coach Rab handed each one of us a cut off t-shirt with that quote screen printed on the back. He even dated the shirt: 1-29-05. We also had shirts that said "TNT"

(Tough, Nasty, and Together) and "Marquette Toughness." Later in the year when we were preparing for postseason play, Rab had a shirt made that said, "One Game Season" on the front, and "Who's Next" on the back. The shirt was designed to mimic the "Untucked" jerseys that Marquette wore in the 1970's and was a nice shout-out to fellow assistant coach, Bo Ellis, who had designed those uniforms. As a player, you loved things like this because no one else had a shirt like that. Students would ask me how they could get a Marquette Toughness shirt, but they weren't for sale. Taglines aside, every guy on the Marquette roster appreciated what those shirts stood for because they were the common thread to our core values as a team. "Marquette Toughness" was meaningless unless you had been through workouts with Scott, been run into the ground by Crean, or been forced to complete that essay at two in the morning and then get back up at 5:00 a.m. for strength and conditioning.

The word "toughness" had come to take on a new meaning as well. There was no denying that every guy on our team was physically tough: you simply can't play at that level without physical toughness. But, Marquette Toughness came to embody the mental grit that accompanies the day-to-day discipline required to thrive in our program. What once seemed like an impossible daily schedule slowly became the norm for every guy on our team. Getting through the day was something I no longer thought about. Rather, my mindset had become, *How do I maintain a consistent intensity and level of excellence in everything I do?*

As if we weren't tough enough, we began practice that week by having the walk-ons take charges as the scholarship guys drove to the basket from different angles. Time after time, guys would drive the ball hard, and there would be a collision near the basket. I'd glance over at Crean, hoping the look on my face would somehow magically move us to the next drill. "Again!" he barked.

We went into our game with St. Louis knowing that they wanted to slow the pace down, but I don't think any of us could've anticipated how slow. At halftime, we led 22-20. Travis was out for the second game in a row, so we desperately needed scoring, and Steve Novak stepped up. Steve stood 6'10" and had one of the purest shooting strokes I had ever seen. During a drill called "Five-minute threes," one guy would shoot as many three-pointers as they could in five minutes, while their partner rebounded. Rebounding for Steve was easy because I could literally stand under the basket, and I kid you not, Steve made 73 out of 75 threes during that drill one day.

Back in St. Louis, Steve finished with a game high 23 points, including five threes, and we emerged in double overtime, 55-51. To play fifty minutes of basketball and only score 55 points was concerning to every Marquette fan, but to persevere and keep playing, even when the shots weren't falling, was a testament to how we were coached. Guys were absolutely exhausted when that final buzzer sounded, but this was Marquette Toughness personified. Our team wasn't built to win games, 100-80. But, we would defend, rebound, claw, and hustle from end line to end line. Winning a dog fight like that on the road after losing three in a row meant a lot to our team.

Injuries are a part of every sport, but it's always disappointing to sustain an injury when your body is in peak physical form. Travis had been injured on and off the entire season, which often resulted in him missing practice. To his credit, he still managed to play at a high level, despite limited repetitions.

Late in the season, we were hosting Louisville and were in a position to make the NCAA tournament. Less than a month earlier, we had gotten whooped, and any chance of us being more competitive started with containing the guard tandem of Larry O'Bannon and Taquan Dean. O'Bannon was one of the most physically impressive basketball players I had ever seen. His upper body was chiseled, and his calves looked like he lived in the weight room. Dean had longer arms and didn't have the bulk of O'Bannon but was also in tremendous shape. Coach Rick Pitino had an interesting way of conditioning players if they made mistakes during practice. Rather than have the whole team run, he would send guys to the sideline, where a set of treadmills awaited them. There, they would run high-speed treadmill sprints until he told them to come back onto the practice floor. I had the opportunity to meet the Louisville strength and conditioning coach before the game, and he looked like a competitor from the World's Strongest Man competitions.

Going back to Travis, everyone on the team knew he was battling a sore ankle, yet we were tied with a few minutes left with a chance to win the game. On back to back possessions, Travis beat Dean to the hoop and essentially missed point blank lay-ups. We ended up losing the game, 64-61, but this was a tough pill to swallow. Not only was Travis a tremendous finisher in traffic, he had always had a knack for hitting big shots. My high school basketball coach, Gordie Sisson, had been in attendance and commented on Travis's inability to finish down the stretch. Out of respect for Coach Sisson, I listened, but I, as well as everyone else on the team, knew that something was wrong for Travis to miss those shots. For four straight years, every missed lay-up was fifteen push-ups in practice. By Travis's senior year, everyone would be on the ground doing push-ups while Travis was getting additional reps in during finishing drills. The guy could flat out make tough, contested shots, which meant he was never doing push-ups. We lost that day, but I always felt bad about the way that game ended.

Most Marquette fans won't recall Travis's ankle injuries, but they will remember another injury that would ultimately seal the fate of our season. On Tuesday, February 22, we were doing some finishing drills with the perimeter players, which was very common for the start of practice. Coach Wardle had a blocking pad and would make contact with each guy as they attempted to finish from the wing. Travis, having a good time with the drill, hit the pad with his hand as he drove and fell awkwardly. He left the gym but didn't appear to be seriously hurt. In fact, we were all laughing because it appeared that he had fallen on purpose. What began as a joke ended in a broken hand. Crean was devastated and so was everyone else. Immediately after the incident, the Marquette basketball family went on lockdown. Rumors swirled about what happened, how it happened, and what the outcome was. There were even students on campus accusing me of breaking his hand. Eventually, the truth came out in a message board post from one of our student managers, who was immediately released from his duties. Why was Crean so upset? To this day, I'm not really sure. Even going back to my interview with the hometown newspaper, Coach Crean liked to be in 100% control.

For the next two months, we played NIT-level basketball, and that's exactly where we ended up. Without Travis's nearly twenty points per game, we struggled to score the ball, and we ended up scoring only 40 points in a 54-40 defeat to Western Michigan in the first round of the NIT. Fellow walk-on Rob Hanley played some valuable minutes at point guard, but the majority of the ball handling duties actually went to 6'8" Marcus Jackson, who was our starting center! Having Marcus bring the ball up either provided a pressure free trip up the floor or pulled a rim protector away from the basket. Either way, once we entered the half court, we lacked firepower on the offensive end. I remember looking at guys like Joe Chapman and wondering why they weren't being more aggressive. Joe could really score the ball when he wanted to; he reminded me of guys I knew that would show up to Rec League and drop 50-60 points. He just had a knack for putting the ball in the basket. By the end of the season, it seemed like everyone was going through the motions, almost like they felt it was more important to "run" the plays correctly than just play good basketball. We finished the season 19-12, which was disappointing considering our 13-1 start.

# 16

# SPRING CONDITIONING

Following our final game, we were given two weeks off before resuming individual workouts and conditioning. The two weeks were great, although they felt like two days. For guys that are injured or even just nursing aches and pains, the two weeks are often spent in the training room. So much for getting away. Fortunately for me, Marquette's spring break happened to fall during our two-week break, granting me a much-needed week in my hometown of Marshfield, WI. While I hate to admit this, I probably played at least a handful of times during my time at home, even though I mentally needed some time away from the game. It's extremely difficult to go from peak physical condition and then just abruptly stop exercising for two weeks. As much as I told myself that I would not step foot in a gym, I would catch myself doing some sort of physical activity almost every day.

Back in Milwaukee for the second week, I was at a party, and Travis's sister, Brittney, was visiting from Chicago. Brittney and I were the same age, and she played collegiately as well, at Lewis University. The two of us were paired up on a beer pong team, and we eked out a one cup victory over Travis and his teammate. We hugged, cheered, and before I knew it, I turned around to Travis drilling me in the nuts! "Why would you do that?" I yelled at him. Was it the beer pong loss? Was it hugging his sister? Frankly, it was probably a combination of the two, and given Travis's absolute hatred for losing, maybe it shouldn't have surprised me. As if a trance had worn off, he followed me into another room and started to profusely apologize, going so far as to demand that I hit *him* in the nuts!

Following our break, all the returning players were brought into the film room to talk about the spring "season." The spring is a time to work on individual skill development, gain strength in the weight room, and get healthy. Put another way, we were going to see a lot of Scott Holsopple. Because the past season had been our last in Conference USA, this would also mark the first spring for Marquette basketball in the Big East Conference. As players, we were obviously aware of the switch, but the coaching staff made a big deal of it, as posters were displayed throughout the McGuire Center. Giant banners were hung in our practice gym, and Luke Benish, our video coordinator, put together a Big East highlight video that was shown at the meeting. The video itself was well-done, but Luke synced it to one of my favorite rap songs, The Game's "Higher," and big dunks were matched with big beats. We were also shown a highlight film containing clips of the four incoming freshmen that would join us in the summer: Dominic James, Jerel McNeal, Wes Matthews, and Dwight Burke.

Veteran guys in the program knew what to expect, and thus, it came as no shock when workouts seemed to be just as intense as they had been in the fall. The workouts, or "Individuals" as they were called, consisted of four guys at a time. Because of NCAA rules, the coaching staff was only allowed two hours of contact per week with players during the spring season. Always trying to maximize time, Crean split his workouts into three, forty-minute sessions per week. Now, when I say forty minutes, I mean forty minutes of work. Stretching and warming up didn't count as part of the allotted time, and the minute that whistle would blow, it was on.

Scott liked to mix it up with guys during the pre-workout stretching in the hallway. It was mid-afternoon in late March, and myself and three post players were scheduled to hit the floor in about five minutes. Standing there, leaning to the left, stretching out my hips and groin, I couldn't believe what I was witnessing. Scott had tackled one of our post players, wrestled him to the ground, and had him in a headlock. Scott's 5'10" max, wearing a Marquette basketball sweatshirt and sweatpants, and he's got a guy, 6'10", pinned to the ground. "Tap out," he yelled, as if he was seriously trying to win a bout. I changed directions and leaned to the right, while my teammate managed to escape Scott's initial headlock and went back to stretching like the rest of us. Another twenty seconds passed, and Scott went after him again. At that point, the joke was over, and my teammate was visibly distressed. Breaking a sweat himself, Scott finally put him in an unbearable chokehold, which led to a tap on the carpet and a collective sigh of relief from the rest of the group.

A minute later, the whistle blew, and we ran out onto the floor to meet Coach Crean at center court. It would have been pretty funny if our fourth teammate hadn't made it onto the floor. I can imagine Coach Crean looking at us: "Where the hell is _____?" "Oh, him, yeah, Coach Holsopple just put him in a chokehold during stretching, and he's out cold in the hallway."

As in most programs, the spring is about developing individual skills and working on your body. Scott's goal for most of the guys was to add muscle, which meant more lifting and less conditioning. For the first time in my life, I felt really "strong" during the spring of 2005. I was benching 185 lbs. eight to ten times, leg pressing 500+ pounds, and wearing a weighted belt for dips and chin-ups. I could rip off more than twenty chin-ups, which felt great considering I couldn't do ten when I arrived in the fall. Sticking with firsts, I finally started to appreciate Scott and vice versa. I was deathly afraid of the guy from day one, and even during the season, there were nights when I hardly slept knowing that I had to get up at 5:30 a.m. for a strength and conditioning workout. But, like many things in life, trust takes time and is developed through hard work and commitment. By mid-April, I actually started to embrace Scott, and I appreciated what he was doing to make me better. Scott would still yell at me, but he also started to complement me and would use me to motivate other players: "Willkom has half of the ability that you do, and he is killing you in the bench press!" he'd scream to some of the scholarship guards.

During one early morning lift, Scott challenged me, Ryan Amoroso, and Dan Fitzgerald to a deadlift competition. We had a deadlift machine, which Scott preferred because it was more like a squat machine and was designed to develop explosive leg power. Fitz went first and did well, knocking out 20+ reps. Dan worked hard all the time, rarely talked, and earned every pound on his 6'9" frame since his transfer to Marquette from Tulane. Amoroso was a monster physically, weighing 250+ lbs. I couldn't compete with him in any exercise above the waist, but legs were a different story. Although his legs were twice the size of mine, he was 6'8", which meant it was harder for him to go all the way down for a full repetition. The grips on the machine would often become soaked with sweat, and guys would complain that they could've ripped off three to four more reps, but their grip slipped. As I stood there and watched Amo's hands slip off the handles, Scott looked at me all excited and said, "Somebody's caught a wicked case of PG!" Somewhat confused, I looked at him and responded, "PG?" "Yeah," he said, "pussy grip." Amoroso beat Fitz by a slight margin, and Scott joked, but in a mocking tone, "Willkom will be lucky to get fifteen." I'm a buck seventy soaking wet, but I grabbed the grip, determined to beat Amo. When you play at Marquette, you compete, in everything. I got to ten, and I felt a sense of strength that wasn't there six months ago. Fifteen. Twenty. Twenty-Five. Thirty. Knowing I had beat Amo was good enough for me, but I kept going, as Scott yelled, with a thrill of excitement in his voice. "Come on Johnny, thirty-five, get thirty-five!" Scott was crouched down in a squat, in his full sweat suit, with an almost psychotic look of excitement in his eyes. My legs burned like no other, but

I knocked out another. "31!" he screamed, followed by "35, 35!" After thirty-four repetitions and hanging on to those handles for dear life, my grip slipped, and it was over. Scott was going crazy, parading around the weight room, while I struggled to even take a step away from the machine. I was a champion for one day, in one meaningless competition, and yet I had won something that I was expected to lose. That was my experience at Marquette in a nutshell: every day was a battle to be won or lost, and most of the time I would lose to bigger, stronger, and faster athletes. Yet, it was that constant quest to maximize my ability that kept me going.

I should mention that team weight workouts were never dramatized like you see in the movies. Maximum effort doesn't allow for you to hoot and holler; you literally have *nothing* left. Any fantasies that people have of going crazy after a huge lift are absolutely false in real life. You want to know what maximum effort looks like? It's an athlete laying on the floor, doing everything they can to catch their breath, feel their limbs, and pick themselves back up.

Two weeks later, I was eating dinner at Schroeder dormitory's dining hall, when some of the men's soccer players came up to me and said, "Man, you must be killing it in the weight room." I stopped mid-bite. "Why would you say that?" I asked. They continued, "Scott told us this morning before we started lifting that not one guy on our team works half as hard as Willkom." I smiled. "There's no way he said that, but thanks."

Whether the comment was true or not, it affirmed what I had felt for weeks: that Scott did respect me. To think that I had won him over was wrong. For six months, I had shown up every day and learned what "maximum effort" truly meant. Maximum effort had nothing to do with how tall I was or my recruiting ranking coming out of high school. It came from the heart and had to be earned, one day at a time. I almost tear up thinking about those workouts and how brutal they were. The days when I did things that I never thought I could do. The times when I didn't think "one more" was humanly possible. I had become a walk-on warrior. For the rest of my life, I'll never experience physical pain like I did in that weight room. And yet, Scott got it out of me. He pushed me to be the best.

# 1 7

# SPRING WORKOUTS

Spring workouts began, and Crean was refreshed. It's almost like his outlook had shifted 360 degrees. It was the middle of March, and we were officially beginning next season, even though next season was seven months away. Due to graduating seniors and injuries, we didn't have a lot of guys to work out in the spring. In fact, on some days, we hardly had the eight guys needed for two groups. The NCAA allowed teams to conduct offseason workouts in groups of four. I rotated between the guards and bigs, getting more out of the perimeter sessions but learning a lot about post philosophy and how we (guards) could make the posts' jobs easier. I worked on feeding the post from different angles and understanding where each guy preferred to catch the ball. We worked on outlet passing, boxing out, and post/perimeter matchups.

My favorite drill was getting a pass on the wing to mimic a fast break and attacking a post player in the lane at full speed. After a few possessions, I realized that Ousmane was sagging way off me, and I hit a couple ten-foot jumpers, with him basically standing under the hoop. "Drive the ball, damnit," Crean yelled. "Play some defense Ousmane," I mumbled to myself. I took it at Ousmane, time after time, working on floaters with both hands, reverse layups, and head fakes in the lane. Growing up in Marshfield, WI, I never got to practice those types of shots against someone 6'10". Mike

Kinsella joked afterwards that I had to be "beat" from drive after drive, but I never thought about it that way. Although this drill was geared to develop the big guys' defense in the lane, it was exactly the type of practice against a live defender that I believed to be the most beneficial. Oftentimes, the post guy would have to get three stops in a row to get out of the drill. I was the designated driver. At one point, I continued to put moves on Ousmane, scoring every other possession and resetting his stop total to zero. Crean loved it, and Wardle would jeeringly yell, "Get 'em Willkom," in a tone straight from an urban playground game. Ouse and I were friends, but in all sports, the minute we started playing, there was no mercy. When Ouse finally got his stops, I nonchalantly offered a fist pound, and he pounded back without saying a word. Next!

Perimeter workouts were a different story. I was not a Division 1 caliber shooter, and it was tough to compete with guys like Steve Novak during shooting drills (Steve would go on to play eleven NBA seasons). Catching fire for me was like Steve getting warmed up. Talk about depressing. Still, my heart knew there was only one way to turn a weakness into a strength: work at it. Curling screens, fading, popping back off screens, we took these shots every day. I didn't become a great shooter, but I became a better shooter, which is what the spring was all about.

I also learned that there were certain things that I couldn't change. I couldn't change the fact that my release was slightly in front of my face rather than in front of my right eye. My elbow simply wasn't in a straight line. Understanding this, however, was my first step to improvement. Rather than change a stroke that was flawed for fifteen years, I worked at becoming more consistent. Shoot the same way every single time. Develop a consistent release point and trajectory. Focus on the same part of the rim every single time. Improve your balance simply by stepping one-two on every shot. I watched Steve and Joe Chapman and picked up on little things like shot preparation, hand placement, and consistent lower body movement. More importantly, in any competition, athletes that don't step up to their level of competition get downright embarrassed. If Joe made seven of ten threes from the wing, I better make at least five, otherwise I didn't deserve to be working out in the same gym.

On the other end of the spectrum, my biggest offensive strength was my ball handling. I could handle the ball, change direction quickly, and get by people. Full court ball handling drills were easy for me because I had grown up with the same drills and been doing them all my life. I would fly through these drills, and Chapman would stare at me, as if to say, *Slow the hell down.* I didn't know any other way, and it didn't make any sense for me to slow down in ball handling if Steve was going to make 95% of his three-point shots. Give a little, take a little, that's competition.

We worked a lot on ball screens and how to read them off the dribble. If the defense goes underneath, you pull the three-ball. If the defense fights over the top, you turn the corner. On a switch, you draw the post player out, then take him one on one. If the switch isn't tight, you dribble split through the two defenders and get to the lane. We did these same drills time after time, and repetition led to instinctively being able to make the right play. By the end of April, I had vastly improved my dribble split reads and could get to the rim in one split dribble from the wing. I would often go so fast that Crean looked at me one day and proclaimed, "Johnny Blur." "We're going to start calling you, Johnny Blur." The nickname was born, and I slept that night dreaming about pick and roll basketball.

Rick Majerus, the legendary Utah coach, would often stop by and watch spring workouts. Rick was a large man that weighed well over 300 lbs., with a balding hairline and thin-framed glasses. Rick was broadcasting for ESPN at the time and would spend the summers in Milwaukee caring for his mother. One day following a workout, I was using one of the urinals in the men's locker room. As I stood there, Rick walked in and positioned himself in front of the urinal right next to me (there were at least four urinals, all unoccupied). Not only was he right next to me, but he proceeded to drop his pants to the ground and stood there in silence. In front of the urinals were mirrors, as well as a large mirror behind us in front of the sinks. As I looked up, I just saw this giant ass and could only smile. We proceeded to wash our hands together, and he said, "You do a nice job out there."

By the end of April, I was a chiseled 175 pounds. I had entered the program at 159, and it felt good to be strong. I had a new nickname, was going on some dates with my crush from Mashuda Hall, and life was good.

Travis had been preparing for the NBA draft and would occasionally join a workout. For the most part, though, all of his work was separate from the rest of the team. At the NBA combine in May, he'd only bench press one rep (at 185 lbs.), and his standing vertical jump of 24.5 inches was one of the lowest of those tested. I bring this up not to rip Travis but to highlight what a tremendous basketball player he was. Despite the physical limitations, Travis would be selected in the second round of June's NBA draft, #38 overall, by the Orlando Magic. His draft party wasn't in some fancy, urban club, but took place at The Press Box, the sports bar owned by his father in Fond du Lac, WI. The NBA is made up of the 491 best players in the world, and I had just spent every day of the last year guarding one of them. Travis had a moxie about him, a swagger that presents itself when a person's confidence never wavers. He was tremendously skilled; don't get me wrong. But, his competitiveness is ultimately what separated himself from everyone else. It was almost as if he had lost a game as a child and vowed to never let it happen again. He was one of the few guys in the country that nobody wanted to play against because of his almost maniacal need to win.

Beginning a post workout one day, we started with a few drills, and then Crean absolutely went berserk. April was about getting stronger and not being in tip top shape, remember? Yet, we got blasted about our conditioning. Crean was so mad that he kicked Chris Grimm, Mike Kinsella, Ousmane Barro, and myself all out of the gym. When a coach tells you to leave, you look at your teammates, as if to imply, *Is he serious?* But he was serious all right. I walked into the locker room, and immediately Coach Strohm burst through the door and yelled, "We are going to get in shape!"

We jogged up the steps and out the front doors of the McGuire Center, which surprised me a bit because we hadn't ever worked out outside on campus before. Strohm said we were going running, and he led a fast pace over to the twelfth street parking garage. When we arrived at the base, we were given instructions to sprint the inclines, then jog the flat straightaways, until we made it to the top of the parking structure. Remember that I was with Chris Grimm, Mike Kinsella, and Ousmane Barro, all guys that stood 6'10" or taller. I blew through the first incline, and Kinsella wasn't happy. "Come on Willkom," obviously suggesting to slow down. *You can outlift me, but I should slow down for you?* Not today Mike. In full attack mode, I raced up the remaining four or five inclines until I saw Wardle at the top. Grimm ran hard and wasn't too far behind. Strohm arrived shortly after via the steps, shirt neatly tucked into his shorts, and was visibly disgusted that I didn't look tired. "Everybody here has a ton of talent, except for Willkom, and you guys don't begin to explore it because you're not in shape!" he muttered. No talent. Thanks Coach. Up next was a distance run through campus, and he made it clear that nobody better fall behind. Fueled by his comments, I drafted right behind Strohm's back, at one point passing him along Wisconsin Avenue. "Stay with the group!" he yelled. No talent. We ran from the parking structure, up to about Taco Bell on 22nd, then headed back down Wisconsin Avenue. By the time we made it back, we were obviously over our forty-minute allotted workout time by the NCAA. Strohm's gray t-shirt was soaked, and he struggled to breathe, while explaining how we had to work hard like that all the time. Even being "out of shape," I stood there thinking, *Work hard? This guy has no idea how easy that was.*

The following week, my one o'clock class got out late, and I arrived at the locker room with five minutes to spare before our individual workout was slated to begin. I threw my jersey and shorts on, then opened the drawer in my locker to grab my shoes. To my surprise, my shoes were absolutely covered in mud! *What in the hell?* I scrambled into the bathroom area and tried to wipe them off in the sink. While they looked a bit better, they were still just terrible looking. Knowing I couldn't be late, I tied them up and ran into the gym, where the other three guys were already huddled up. "What the hell happened to your shoes?" said Joe Chapman. Before I could even respond, Crean appeared, looked at me with a bewildered look on his face and simply said, "Go change your shoes."

I found out later that Travis had taken my shoes to go mudding, or at least that's what he said. Andy Klister, our team manager, begrudgingly took me into the equipment room and handed me a brand-new pair of Nike's. For whatever reason, it didn't seem like he believed my story, but Andy also guarded that equipment room with his life so maybe he had other plans for those shoes. Regardless, it was one of the few times that the staff was reminded that we were college kids. 99% of the time, it was all business, and even though my heart was pounding at the thought of being late, I smiled as I walked home that day, knowing that deep down, we were all goof balls with teenage personalities.

# 18

# BELGIUM

Spring workouts finished up, and I was excited because in early May, I left for Antwerp, Belgium, to take a three-credit international business course. I had always wanted to "study abroad," but given my choice to be a student athlete, I understood that it wasn't realistic for me to ever spend an entire semester outside of the USA. So, when I had the opportunity to pursue this three-week program, I jumped at it. Life in Belgium was much more relaxed, but we still had class every day at 8 a.m.

As part of the program, we got to tour the Ford proving grounds in Lommel, Belgium. The proving grounds had more than sixty road surfaces from around the world and employed retired race car drivers to test drive vehicles all day. I was given an opportunity to ride in a mini-van, through a closed, wooded course, paved with cobblestone. The road itself was slick from varying intensities of artificial rain. Our driver spoke limited English but seemed nice enough. Almost immediately after he started driving, I felt a knot in my stomach, a nervousness that I hadn't experienced in quite a while. Approaching a sharp turn, with woods on both sides of a single lane, the driver sped up and whipped the van to the left. I got that weird sensation in my stomach when you're about to tip over. I kept telling myself that there's no way I'd be allowed in this van if there was a strong chance of a crash but still held on to the "Oh shit" bar for dear life. When the ride was finished, we thanked our driver and were later told that he would drive more than fifty other cars on that course before the end of the day.

After the woods course, we were led over to a race track in the center of the proving grounds. A man pulled up in a silver Aston Martin, rolled down the window, and said, "Get in." I can't remember how fast we were going because my neck was glued to the passenger seat. Needless to say, it was the fastest vehicle I had ever been in by a long shot. I wish I could've appreciated the ride more, but the force at that speed pinned me against the seat.

Following the rides, we were part of an international business discussion in a large, stadium style seating room that displayed world flags up on the walls. It looked like a room for Congress, and each seat had an individual microphone and nameplate. Executives from Ford explained that top-to-top summits, along with international relations meetings were held in that room.

In addition to the Ford facility, we traveled to Paris, Amsterdam, and Rome. To see some of those famous churches and landmarks was absolutely amazing. The fact that Rome had been built on top of itself and still had underground tunnels and remnants at every turn just fascinated me. Robin Williams was talking to Matt Damon about the Sistine Chapel in *Good Will Hunting*, and he famously asked, "Do you know what it smells like?" Seeing it with your own eyes, smelling the air, and just taking it all in is truly something to behold.

I tried hard to stay in shape during my time there. Almost every day, I went on runs, and it was a great way for me to see the city of Antwerp. In fact, in a somewhat legendary story, I got lost running and ended up in this warehouse district where I saw a sign for a large "rave" happening later that evening. "Do you know how to get to the University of Antwerp?" I'd stop and ask people on the street. The first two folks simply smiled and pointed in a direction; the third guy smiled, pointed, and then said, "That way." At that point, three pieces of feedback gave me some confidence. When I finally arrived back on campus, I told a teacher where I had been, and she figured I had run more than thirteen miles.

My fellow classmates were intrigued by the rave idea, and later that night, it became one of the weirdest things I had ever experienced. People dancing solo, glow sticks everywhere, and lots of ecstasy. In fact, it probably wasn't weird at all; I'm just not a "rave" guy!

When I returned to the United States, my plan was to work a few Marquette basketball camps but to also work some of my own Playmakers camps. Mike and I still had a well-attended summer camp circuit, and I loved being around those camps because they were something I had helped build. It also meant a great deal to continue the legacy of Dave Macarthur, who would've been so proud to see the hundreds of smiling kids in attendance. As if I needed any more motivation, there was something special about returning to those small towns because I was one of those smiling kids ten years before that. To be able to do some unique things with the basketball and share that with those kids and communities meant a lot to me.

I had only been in Milwaukee for a day or two, and Marquette's first camp of the summer was slated to begin. I showed up bright and early and was excited to see the guys and meet the kids. Teaching young kids how to play basketball is a passion of mine and probably always will be. Having been out of the fold for a few weeks, it was a bit of an eye opener when an hour into camp, Crean had all of us players go through an hour long "demonstration" for the kids. This was essentially a practice, but because we weren't allowed to have practice, sessions were weaved into the daily camp schedule. Having not touched a basketball in three weeks, I admittedly struggled. My lungs were fine; I just wasn't in basketball shape, and my timing was off. Following that workout, the kids were dispersed to different gyms for game time. Before I could leave the court, though, Crean stopped me and let me know how he felt about my performance. "You were fucking terrible. Do they not have fucking basketballs in Europe?" he barked. I knew better than to argue so I sheepishly acknowledged that I needed to get in better shape, and we went our separate ways.

For the first time in my life, I felt used. I had gone to Europe to expand my world view. For the previous eight months, I had spent every day going balls to the wall for the Marquette basketball program. My trip to Belgium wasn't about abandoning Marquette basketball. In fact, it was almost exactly what Crean had been preaching all year: better yourself and compete in everything you do. I went to Europe to get ahead in school, learn about the world, and take advantage of the one time I could go without missing any organized basketball activities.

When the campers went home for the day, I spent about three hours putting myself through drills, and this would continue for the next five days. By the end of the week, I felt better physically, but my mind was still fragile. I felt an immense pressure to get back to peak form as soon as possible. Several high school coaches from Chicago told me after camp that I would compete for playing time in the fall. Regardless, my spirits were down, but I kept telling myself that going to Europe had absolutely been the right choice. And even if it had been the wrong one, I was proud of myself for having made a decision that I felt was in my best interest. Did Coach Crean truly care about what was best for me? I'll probably never know.

One paradox that I'll never understand is that if a young athlete needs to get in shape, most parents will tell them to run a bunch of miles. While it may improve their endurance, the only way to get in shape for any sport is to train hard with sport-specific movements. To clarify, I'm not advocating playing a single sport, but I'm emphasizing that basketball players don't move like distance runners. They start, stop, slide, jump, back pedal, etc. It's the reason why an athlete that ran fifty miles last week feels out of shape during this week's basketball game. Sounds obvious, yet I bring it up because I've heard it so many times from adults.

Back to Marquette, I worked camp again the following week,

and we had Dan Hurley in town to help with "demonstrations." Hurley played at Seton Hall and is now the head coach at UConn. His brother, Bobby, obviously had a remarkable career at Duke and now coaches at Arizona State. His father, Bob, was the long-time coach at St. Anthony's High School in New Jersey and is a member of the Basketball Hall of Fame.

Unlike the previous week, my body was starting to adjust to basketball again, and my timing was much better. More importantly, I liked Dan Hurley a lot. He coached me, pushed me, and was very vocal during full court finishing drills. When our workouts were over, he sat down next to me and said, "You do a hell of a job." Little did he know, but I needed that confidence boost, given the events of the previous week.

Following that second week of camp, I returned to my hometown of Marshfield and proceeded to work Playmakers camps as planned. Although I was demonstrating many of the same drills that I had done thousands of times, I felt appreciated being back in my hometown. What wasn't good enough two weeks prior was now an incredible highlight for many of the campers. We ended camp that week with hundreds of kids gathered in a circle, and I did a drill called "Kill the Grass," motivated by the applause and cheers coming from the campers and their parents. I connected with friends, made some new ones, and for the first time in quite a while, I felt a bit of balance return to my life.

In early August, I joined some friends at a Wednesday night church service at Believer's Church, simply to see a different perspective than a traditional Catholic mass. As I sat there and prayed, I realized that I needed to make a change. This wasn't a spontaneous idea that the good Lord had just planted, but something I had been thinking about the entire summer. After the service ended, I stood in the parking lot and dialed Coach Crean's cell phone number. "Ring, ring, ring." It went to voicemail, and I simply said, "Hey coach, it's John Willkom and was just hoping to chat for a minute." Click.

I had never called Coach Crean. I almost breathed a sigh of relief when he didn't answer, but less than thirty seconds passed, and he was calling back. "Hello," I said. "Hey John, it's Coach Crean. What's up?" In that moment, I took a deep breath and just thought, *Be honest and speak from the heart.* I proceeded to tell him that I was really hoping to have this conversation in Milwaukee, but he assured me now was a good time. I explained that my heart just wasn't in it anymore, and that I felt I would be doing the team a disservice with that type of mindset. I told him I wanted to pursue a business internship and maybe try coaching, but that it had been an honor and privilege to be a part of the Marquette basketball program. Crean, calm and collected, thanked me and said he appreciated me thinking about the team and how much he admired my hard work and commitment to Marquette.

Just like that, it was over. For twenty-one years, basketball had consumed me. Over the past year, I had spent almost every waking minute training for, playing, watching, studying, or reading about basketball. For the first time in several years, my body felt fresh. No more sprained fingers, sore feet, legs, or back. There would be no more 6:00 a.m. conditioning, no more Crean, and no more Boston Market. I had left on my own accord, and while some may have called me a quitter, I knew better than that. The physical results of being pushed so hard eventually fade, but the mental grit to get through anything stays with you for life.

Steve Novak would later tell my brother, Kyle, "I don't know how your brother did it." "What do you mean?" asked Kyle. "I just mean, it would've been so hard to go through a season like that if I hadn't been playing," said Steve.

So, why did I do it? Ultimately, I can say I wanted to better myself and maximize my ability. I knew I was maturing as a man, and I would take the work ethic and discipline from my time as a player to everything I did moving forward. At my very core, though, I played basketball at Marquette University because I truly loved the game. I loved being around the gym and being surrounded by people who shared that passion. I loved being coached by elite coaches and the preparation that went into game planning. I loved the attention to detail by our student managers, who would neatly lay out my practice gear *every* day! When you love something, it never leaves you. And although it would take on a different persona moving forward, that love for the game, while slightly dampered, would find a flame soon enough.

# 1 9

# MOVING ON

My basketball journey was far from over, but I wasn't sure what the next step would be. I was a junior in college, 21 years old, and had five of the coolest roommates on campus: Marc Dettmann, who had competed for a walk-on spot a year earlier, Mark Johnson, Rob Mallof, Greg Jackson, and Matt McDonnell. One day on our way to class, I was telling Dettmann that I had contacted some Milwaukee area high school coaches about possibly helping out during the upcoming season. He immediately asked me if I had reached out to Dave Cooks, who had been his high school coach at Milwaukee Marquette High School. I told him I hadn't, and he proceeded to tell me all the reasons why I should go work for Coach Cooks.

Cooks and I exchanged a few emails, and I was scheduled to meet with him the following week. Marquette University High School is about eighteen blocks north of Marquette University. During the fall, it's walkable, but given that I had a university-issued bus pass, I figured I'd take the bus. I sat down in a classroom outside of Coach Cooks' office, and he came in and said, "hello," and then asked, "Could you go get me some water?" *No problem*, I thought. When I returned holding the cup from the top, he looked at me like I was crazy and told me to get him a different glass because I had touched the part where he would be drinking. We briefly chatted about basketball and my class schedule. He then left the room, and I took the bus back to campus.

"How'd it go?" asked Marc Dettmann when I walked into our apartment. I didn't really know how to respond. On one aspect, I was thankful that Dettmann had introduced me, but all the great characteristics that Dettmann admired about Cooks definitely hadn't shone through in that first meeting. "I'm not really sure what he thinks of me," I said. I told him about the water thing, and he just laughed, while explaining that Cooks liked to mess with people. *Ok*, I thought, *but he had just met me for the first time!* Rob Mallof, one of our other housemates, had just walked in and stood by the kitchen as we talked. Rob had also attended Marquette High and had been a team manager for Cooks. "Johnny," he said, "you're going to love Cooks."

I accepted a varsity assistant coaching position with Cooks, and despite my reservations, trusted Marc and Rob's opinions. We absolutely underwent a "feeling out" period, but the more time I spent at Marquette High, the more Coach Cooks seemed to open up. For starters, Coach was in a wheelchair and had been since the age of fifteen, when he suffered a spinal aneurism and was left paralyzed from the waist down. To any onlooker, it was clear that Coach was different. But, it wasn't just the wheelchair that made him different; it was his whole outlook on life. You could tell that he had a reason for living, probably because there were times when his life had almost been taken away. Cooks was a devout Christian, and he would proudly make references to his faith in conversation, during practice, and in interviews. He'd even play Christian rap music during conditioning for the kids.

Like Crean, practices with Cooks were tough, and the kids ran a lot. What stood out about Cooks, though, was that everyone in the program was held to a higher moral standard. Specifically, there was no swearing, no cursing, no disrespectful behavior, period. Unlike with Crean, where I probably heard the word "fuck" more than 10,000 times in a year, Cooks would make you run for *every letter*. And not just players, but coaches, managers, everyone. I let an F bomb slip one day and immediately knew what I had done. Thinking I would just apologize, I took responsibility and said, "My bad, I didn't mean that." Cooks just stared at me, emotionless, and said, "Get on the line." "But..." I stammered. He blew the whistle, and before I could say another word, I just started running suicides, wind pants and all, one for every letter.

Occasionally, the players would be running sprints at the end of practice, and the student managers would pull a base drum out of a storage closet. Sitting Indian-style against the backstop behind the basket, one of them would pound that drum as the kids ran. "Keep the beat," Cooks would tell them.

My class schedule was still from 8 a.m. to about 1 p.m. every day, so I would head to Marquette High School around 2:45 p.m. each day to talk with Cooks in his office and get ready for practice at 3:30. One day, we were sitting there, and he said, "You want some juice?" "Um, I guess, sure," I said. He opened this mini fridge under his desk and pulled out a container of Dole Mango Pineapple. To say Cooks liked juice was an understatement. He poured me a glass and made me grab it (so he wouldn't touch the top). After I took a few sips, he got all giddy, and with his big, bright smile exclaimed, "That's some stuff right there!" I drank a lot of juice in that office. Occasionally, he'd mix in some cranberry or grape, but he sure loved that mango pineapple.

After Cooks' spinal aneurism, he was no longer able to play high school basketball. But in true Cooks fashion, he played wheelchair basketball at the University of Wisconsin-Whitewater. He eventually went on to get his MBA at Duke, where he was a team manager for legendary coach Mike Krzyzewski and helped them win two national titles in the early 1990's. After finance jobs out east, he eventually returned home to Milwaukee to coach at his alma matter, teach AP economics, and lead the school's diversity program.

Cooks' office had all types of memorabilia, books, media guides, and other things that caught the eye. It was one of those offices that made it hard to pay attention because you always found yourself looking at something else that you hadn't noticed before. Some of my favorites were the posters from previous Duke teams, a letter from then Tennessee coach, Buzz Peterson, and a picture of himself with Michael Jordan and former Milwaukee Buck, Terry Cummings.

The coaching staff at Marquette High was something else. Percy Eddie was 6'10" and had played at Kansas State, along with some short stints in the NBA. Mark Briggs, a University of Wisconsin Milwaukee alum, stood 6'5" and could really shoot the ball. He'd famously tell kids, "Hit a shot before you graduate!" At practice, I would work with the point guards, Briggs with the wing players, and Eddie with the big guys. To have this type of experience at the high school level was a huge advantage for the kids, and I enjoyed watching Eddie and Briggs coach, as they taught things that you only see done in the professional ranks. I asked those guys one day why they were coaching at Marquette High, and they both pointed to Cooks and said, "That guy right there." I didn't know Percy and Mark the way I knew Coach Cooks, but they would often allude to Cooks' mentorship: personally, professionally, and spiritually. The longer I was there, I began to feel the same way. Sure, I was coaching a basketball team and working with high school kids who all had dreams of being where I had just been. The difference, though, is that I was also being coached, and there wasn't a day in that office from 2:45-3:30 that we didn't talk about ethical living, dating, family, college, or society.

Right after Christmas, Cooks had scheduled us to play in a holiday tournament at Brebeuf Jesuit High School in Indianapolis. We were slated to play Andrean High School from Merrillville, IN, who had this brute of a man on their roster who was apparently committed to Notre Dame. Watching this guy warm up, I honestly recall thinking that he must be a football recruit because of his wide build. At 6'7", 245 lbs., he made the guys on our team look like small children. It didn't take long to realize that this guy was indeed a basketball recruit. Luke Harangody, or "Gody" as his teammates called him, scored from all over the place. He could shoot threes, maneuver in the post, and was an excellent free throw shooter. Notre Dame coach Mike Brey was on hand for the game and for good reason. We battled them close, due in large part to our senior leader, Dan Landisch, who went back and forth with Harangody in the second half before eventually running out of gas. Harangody would go on to have one of the most decorated careers in the history of Notre Dame basketball, finishing as the school's all-time second leading scorer (2,476 points) and rebounder (1,222), before bouncing around the NBA as an undersized power forward. Our own Dan Landisch would go on to play at Fordham.

While the loss hurt, one thing that I always admired about Cooks was that he viewed being a part of the team as more than just basketball. By that, I mean that he wanted the kids to have experiences, try new things, and be challenged off the court. That night, we had a legendary meal at Maggiano's, and several kids tried oysters, calamari, and a variety of other things for the first time. Rich or poor, black or white, every guy had a seat at the table, and our team was close because of the coaching staff's effort to coordinate events like this. In early February, Cooks hosted a Super Bowl party at his house for the entire team, and guys were treated to his famous wings. At the end of the season, we finished right around .500, but I'll never forget guys like Matt Erbe and Danny Fox, seniors who hardly played the entire season but openly expressed their gratitude and sincere appreciation to have been a part of that team.

I learned an important lesson from Coach Cooks that will remain with me for the rest of my life, and it all centered around culture. Creating the right culture sustains people through the highs and lows, and it all starts with leadership. Win or lose, there was a way in which we did things at Marquette High that set the tone for everything we did. When you have a culture of respect, hard work, being on time, and good sportsmanship, it doesn't just change the way players perform on the basketball court, it sets them up for a lifetime of success.

Following the season, my housemates and I were hosting a party one night on campus. I figured it wouldn't be too rowdy early on, so I invited Coach Cooks over for some BBQ, as I knew it was one of his favorites. He showed up around 7 p.m. to a packed apartment. There were probably a few more people over than I had anticipated, but if Coach Cooks had a strength, he could walk into a crowded room of strangers and build an instant rapport. The guys operating the grill had been a little distracted talking to our female friends, and it would be another forty-five minutes or so before any of the food would be ready. Cooks looked at my housemates, and then he looked at me: "A brother can't get no eats when there's flesh in the crib?" "What?" they replied with confused looks on their faces. I knew exactly what he meant and started to laugh as he hollered out, "Oohh!" We finally did get him his food, and he must've talked to every one of my friends, while reminding me more than once that it was "hotter than a mug" in my apartment.

# 20

# INTERNSHIPS

All winter long, I had been working to secure an internship for the summer. While the door was always open to work Playmakers basketball camps, I wanted to get out of my comfort zone and learn something new. At the time, I was most interested in sports marketing (along with every other college-aged male), and I had been interviewing with Lammi Sports Management, which had a small office in the Third Ward of the city. Brian Lammi had started the company on the coattails of his relationship with Brad Johnson, the former NFL quarterback, who had led the Tampa Bay Buccaneers to a Super Bowl championship in 2003. Brian was Brad's agent, and by 2006, he had secured marketing and sponsorship deals for more than a hundred professional athletes. About a week after my interview, Dan Cary, who was Brian's partner in the business, called to offer me a part-time internship. Essentially, they were going to hire two interns and have one work from 8-noon and the other from 1-5 p.m. each day. I was psyched, but the internship was unpaid, so I knew I'd need to find another job.

In typical Coach Cooks fashion, he connected me to the Vice President of M&I bank. When I arrived for my interview, he walked me to a corner office on the top floor of a downtown high rise. I was blown away by the view, as you could see parts of Marquette's campus, as well as Lake Michigan in the opposite direction. We had a great chat (mostly about my basketball experiences), and a couple weeks later, I was offered a job as a bank teller at a branch off of 27th and National. I'd work at Lammi from 8-noon and then book it over to the bank to work from 1-5 p.m. The bank required me to wear a shirt & tie, which I was actually excited about because it made me feel like a professional.

As I finished my junior year of college and got ready to start, it occurred to me that I hadn't thought through how I would get to Lammi, then to the bank, and home again at the end of each day. I didn't have a car, and my bus pass wasn't valid during the summer because I wasn't in school. After talking to my roommates, Marc Dettmann told me he had an old bike at his parents' house that he could bring down if I wanted to use it. For the next three months, I'd roll my dress pants up into my dress socks, throw on my backpack, and bike downtown to Lammi Sports. At noon, I'd scarf down a home-made sandwich and book it to the bank. I needed to bike fast to get there in time, but I tried as hard as I could not to get too sweaty. Needless to say, biking in ninety-degree heat every day in dress clothes led to quite a few "paper towel baths" once I got to the bank. On multiple occasions, my chain would fall off my bike, and I'd pull and yank on that thing, trying not to get grease on my nice clothes. Despite the occasional hiccup, I was never late and was truly excited to serve the customers of that bank in the best way possible.

I learned so much that summer, but one of the major highlights was working Donald Driver's football camp. Driver was a star wide receiver for the Green Bay Packers, and his shiny, white teeth and big smile made him a fan favorite. Brian Lammi was Donald's agent and did a tremendous job of connecting him to the local community. Driver had a TV show, was featured in McDonald's commercials, and spoke at a variety of charity events. Brian had asked me if I had any interest in assisting with the camp, and given my experience running camps, of course I did!

Driver presented himself like a normal guy, and mostly because he wasn't afraid to tell you where he had been. I asked him one day if he had ever considered solely training for the Olympics, as he had been an All-American high jumper at Alcorn State. He told me about living out of his car and the times when he had nothing. "Even then," he said, "I knew I was going to play in the NFL." He went on to say that he had never seriously considered training for the Olympics, even though he had high jumped 7'6.5" inches in 1996!

Following camp one day, Driver looked at me, of all people, and said, "Let's get some food!" I jumped into his Hummer, and we headed down to La Perla, which was a popular Mexican restaurant located a few blocks from the bank I worked at. Right after we sat down, I noticed a few guys from Marquette sitting across the way, and they immediately stumbled over, margarita pitchers in hand, and slurred, "Hey Wilks, whoooo's your friend?!"

I was somewhat embarrassed to admit that I knew these fine gentlemen, but Driver laughed it off and actually bought them more margarita pitchers. Later that week, I was with a group of friends on campus, and one of those guys mentioned that he had seen me at La Perla "with some guy wearing dope earrings." Must have been a Bears fan.

I spent the summer assisting Brian and Dan, as they set up marketing activities for their client base. In one memorable week, Brian had me calling Miami and Dallas-based businesses to see if they'd be interested in booking Dan Patrick, the TV/radio personality, for speaking engagements during the NBA finals. After a few calls, Brian called me into his office and said, "How much do you think Dan Patrick is worth?" I paused for a bit, not really understanding the question. "What do you think he's worth to speak for an hour?" he repeated. I looked at him sheepishly, unsure of what to say, and then he proceeded to explain a very valuable lesson: "You need to believe he's worth every penny of what you're asking these businesses to pay. If you don't believe that, you'll never sell anything." I worked all week to try and secure a speaking engagement for Dan but to no avail. The Benihana Restaurant Group had shown the most interest, but I wasn't able to pull it all together in the short time frame.

Meanwhile at the bank, I was performing well and getting faster processing transactions. I worked every Saturday morning as well from 8 a.m. to 1 p.m., and there would literally be lines of people out the door waiting to deposit/cash checks. This wasn't your typical bank, in that it was very transaction heavy, with a lot of cash switching hands. My manager, Teresa, told all of us that we needed to move fast and not spend too much time chatting with customers. I got called into her office one day. "John," she said, "you were not hired to be a financial advisor. You need to stop giving customers financial advice." *Ok*, I thought, *but where's the value-add in that?*

Every week I got faster and cut down on mistakes, and we had an internal contest (unbeknownst to our manager) to see how many transactions each teller could process on a Saturday morning. Following my first win, I dug out a trophy from a back closet that must've been more than thirty years old. It simply read "Teller of the Month." In a comical, yet somewhat serious expression, I placed it next to my name plate and told the other tellers that every Saturday, they would have a chance to win back the trophy. One customer in particular would come in at least twice a week, shake my hand, and exclaim, "My man, teller of the month!" I kept that trophy the rest of the summer.

About two months into my bank job, I was called one day and asked to meet two police detectives on campus. Apparently, I had cashed a fake check on behalf of a customer about a month before that. The questions they asked were rather vague, and I never heard back from them after our meeting.

I worked at the bank until the end of September. Despite being asked to continue working there following my internship, I wanted to coach one more season at Marquette High, so I hung up my dress clothes for my basketball gear once again. In early October, that bank was robbed at gunpoint. Fortunately, no one was hurt, but I felt terrible knowing that all my former teammates had to go through that.

The summer of 2006 is one I'll never forget. Donald Driver, the bank trophy, and biking all over Milwaukee in a shirt and tie were all memorable. But, what really stood out was a random request to help someone in need.

Brian Lammi approached my desk one day in June and said, "John, do you know who Rick Majerus is?" "Of course," I said enthusiastically, knowing the history of Rick's time at Marquette as a coach and his tremendous success at the University of Utah. I also thought back to the last time I had talked to Rick in the Marquette men's basketball locker room and couldn't help but smile. "Well," he said, "I'm doing some marketing work for Rick, and he asked if I could get him an assistant for the summer." Brian explained that Rick was ideally looking for a female, but that he had told him about me and was awaiting a response. Hesitant at first, he eventually agreed.

Rick was in the process of moving into a new condo, and one of my major tasks would be to shine the place up before he moved in. Granted, scrubbing floors wasn't what I originally had in mind, but this was Rick Majerus, and if Rick wanted his condo cleaned, then I was going to clean it. I probably worked for Rick about ten times over a two-month period, but I was so impressed by the way he treated me. His hospitality was unique for a guy so well known that he could get pretty much whatever he wanted. There were several times that Rick brought me lunch or offered me a water or soda. Because I didn't have a car, he'd often pick me up on campus in his Ford Escape. One day as I was leaving an on campus mini-mart, a fellow student stopped me and said, "I swear I saw you get into a car with Rick Majerus on Monday!" "What would Rick Majerus be doing in Milwaukee?" I asked him. "You're right," he said.

Rick had attended Marquette High School and attempted to walk-on at Marquette University in 1967. In Rick's book, *My Life on a Napkin*, Coach Al McGuire (less politely) had told

Rick that he was the worst player he had ever seen. Instead, McGuire allowed Majerus to be a student manager, and shortly after his graduation in 1970, he was hired as an assistant to McGuire in 1971.

Majerus would spend twelve years as an assistant at Marquette, winning a national title in 1977. In 1983, Majerus became Marquette's head coach and held that post until 1986, when he left for the NBA to assist the Don Nelson-led Milwaukee Bucks. After a season with the Bucks, Majerus went back to college, coaching Ball State for two seasons and Utah for fifteen. He left the University of Utah in 2004 after 323 victories to get his health under control.

One day, Rick asked me to meet him at the Pfister Hotel to assist him with moving some items out of his hotel room. Rick wasn't your typical hotel guest. I am not sure how long he had been staying there, but it was over a year, and he occupied two connecting hotel rooms. The day before, he had called and told me to meet him at the room at 10:00 a.m. Easy enough. Yet, when I walked up to his door, I suddenly wasn't sure whether I had the wrong room number because no one came to the door. I didn't want to call and sound irresponsible, so I knocked again: once, twice, and finally a third time. Still, no response. I stood and waited, and not thirty seconds later, Rick came waddling down the hallway soaking wet in a towel and swim cap. The man was 58 years old, 300+ pounds, and rolls of fat layered his mid-section. The top of his head was pretty much bald, so the swim cap seemed a bit unnecessary. Rick had mentioned he was a swimmer, but the stories of his exploits in the water were like my faith in God. I didn't need to see Rick in a Speedo to know that he swam.

"Hey," he said. "I just got done with my morning workout." He had a slight grin on his face, almost bating me into a reaction, but I kept a straight face, not wanting to give him any ammunition. "It's all good," I told him, as I followed him into the adjoining suites. As Rick changed into regular clothes, I was amazed by all the Post-It notes on the walls. There were hundreds of them in every color on multiple walls! Rick had already prepared some boxes for me to take out to his vehicle, so I spent about a half hour going back and forth with boxes in hand. After the last box, Rick sat down with a stack of magazines, and we sorted through each one, dumping the ones he didn't want to keep. Occasionally, I'd see things like hand written game notes or practice plans that perked my interest. "You mind if I keep any of these?" I asked. "No problem," he mumbled, although it was hard to tell if he was even paying attention. There was one document with detailed, hand-written scouting notes from Dino Gaudio, who was then an assistant coach at Wake Forest. As I paged through them, it hadn't even occurred to me that he was no longer sitting next to me.

"You hungry?" he said, standing in the corner of the room. "Sure, why not," I told him. "Good, 'cause I just ordered you a sausage sandwich." *What the hell is a sausage sandwich?* I thought. As much as Rick valued my opinion, food was nonnegotiable, in that he called the shots. Sure enough, about a half hour later, a kid from an Italian deli down the street showed up with a white paper bag full of all kinds of stuff.

Working for Rick made me realize how smart this guy was. Everyone in America could tell you that Rick Majerus knew the game of basketball, but Rick knew a lot more than just basketball. He would occasionally speak about medical procedures or about people he knew, and I would listen intently thinking, *How can some of this be true?* One day I went home after work and "Googled" a few of the names he had dropped in conversation, and sure enough, these were real people that accomplished exactly what he had said.

I moved Rick into his new condo unit on the East Side of Milwaukee and organized several collector items, such as signed merchandise from guys like Michael Jordan, Charles Barkley, and Isiah Thomas. I'd ask him about his former players like Keith Van Horn, Michael Doleac, and Andre Miller, and he spoke so highly about those guys' character and how much he enjoyed coaching them. For all the hell stories I've heard about his time at Utah, here was a man that looked back and appreciated three guys that maximized their talent.

He'd often hand me his cell phone to either write down voice messages or respond to text messages. Often, well-known basketball coaches would leave messages, and when I'd ask him how he wanted me to respond, I'd get some interesting answers depending on the coach. He got an email one day from David Stern, then the commissioner of the NBA. "I'll take care of that one tomorrow," he told me.

I did a lot of odd jobs for Rick. On a Saturday afternoon, I had basically finished scrubbing all the hardwood floors in the condo. The place looked great, and I was proud of the work I had done. "Ya know, I need a water hose for the lawn," he said. He sent me off with some money, and I drove his Escape to the hardware store, where I bought the hose that he had instructed me to buy. I kept thinking to myself that the only "lawn" on Rick's property was about an "8 x 8" sliver of grass near the garage. When I got back, we hooked up the hose, and with a proud look on his face, we watered that little patch of grass.

One day, we were sitting around, and Rick wanted to go through garbage bags of hotel-sized shampoos, lotions, and conditioners. I guess it made sense, since he had been living out of a hotel for most of his adult life. We literally sat there for two hours, and he'd say, "What do you think of this one?" as he'd hand it over, and I'd smell it. We went through hundreds and kept the ones we liked. "Take some of these back to campus for your girlfriends," he told me.

I got a text one day that said, "Can you swing by Usinger's Sausage Company and pick up an order for me?" I biked to Rick's condo, picked up his Ford Escape, and drove over to Usinger's, where I proceeded to pick up eighty-nine pounds of bratwurst. After a month of conversations around healthy eating and exercise, I was buying the most ridiculous amount of sausage I'd ever seen! He told me it was for an event. As I unloaded it into a freezer in his garage, I knew it wasn't for an event.

We got together for dinner one night, and Rick brought a lady friend. This woman was very attractive, smart, witty, and very engaging. I sat there thinking, *How does a guy like Rick end up with a woman like this?* Anyways, towards the end of the meal, our waiter came by and asked if we wanted dessert, to which Rick immediately responded with his order. While we waited, Rick started to gush about the woman sitting across from him. His face lit up, and she blushed as he flattered her with compliments. If there was ever a way to attract a woman, Rick was hitting on all cylinders.

But then, in a single comment, the table went silent. "Sometimes when I think about (woman's name), I just want to eat her!" he said. I smiled, he smiled, and almost as if she was waiting for my reaction, an awkward silence was broken when all three of us started to laugh.

That fall, Rick went back to work for ESPN, as a color commentator for men's college basketball games. During a live broadcast, he responded to Steve Lavin's comments about then UCONN forward Rudy Gay: "Ya know, I'm not a big Gay guy, but I really like those guys that are rock solid." To Lavin's credit, he kept it together, but the clip became a YouTube highlight for years to come. He would later tell Jay Bilas in another comical studio exchange, "Jay, you're probably one of those guys who gets out of the shower when he needs to take a piss."

In April of 2007, Majerus would take the head coaching job at St. Louis University. While I'll never take any credit for his return to the sidelines, my time with him the previous summer illustrated that being around young people seemed to bring out his best self.

As he was introduced at his press conference, he told the crowd regarding his last name. "The name is really from Luxembourg," he said, "and I think it means sausage-eater" ("The Life and Times," 2008, para. 12). He proceeded to field questions from the national media before leaving the Jesuit leadership at St. Louis with a final sound bite. "The greatest mystery of faith to me is not the resurrection or the virgin birth. I want to know if the Corinthians ever wrote back" ("The Life and Times," 2008, para. 12).

Rick Majerus would coach at St. Louis for five seasons, going 26-8 in 2011-2012 and leading his team to the round of 32 in the NCAA Tournament.

On December 1, 2012, Rick Majerus passed away from congestive heart failure. A remarkable personality, leader, and coach, he was 64. May he rest in peace.

# 21

# WRISTS

On Halloween, 2006, I was playing intramural flag football down at Valley Fields, where a variety of Marquette intramural leagues are held. My roommate, Mark Johnson, had put together a team, and the playoffs had begun. Driving down the field, we were in the "red zone," and Mark launched a pass over the middle that I jumped up and tried to pull down. I had run a hard "in" route, and as the ball approached slightly behind me, I leapt up and twisted backwards to try and reel it in. As soon as I reached back, a defender took out my legs, and trying to avoid landing on my head, I extended both of my arms toward the turf to break my fall. Immediately, I heard a loud snap and crashed to the ground, writhing in pain. I had broken both of my wrists: one on the turf and the other on my opposite arm as I tried to brace the fall. As I attempted to sit up, I looked down and could see that my right arm wasn't in a straight line and collapsed back down in a bit of a panic. Marquette's public safety officers arrived and wrapped my arms to my chest with some yellow, pre-wrap, and I was driven to the nearest hospital.

I sat in the emergency room waiting area for more than two hours. One of my housemate's, Rob Mallof, finally approached the desk area and went off at the two women sitting there. "Are you kidding me?" he yelled, "He's got two broken arms!" A few minutes later, I was admitted and wheeled away to an open bed. Lying there, a nurse came in and told me to straighten my right arm. When I told her it was straight, I'll never forget the concerned look on her face. My mother had driven down from Marshfield and had just arrived, and I was happy to see her.

I had two blessings over the course of the next two days that I'll never forget. The first is that Rob's uncle was a renowned surgeon in the Milwaukee area. Rob called him and explained what had happened, and he ended up coming in the next day to operate on both of my wrists. I had broken the radius and ulna on both sides and would have T-shaped titanium plates put in to keep the bones together.

The second blessing came from my friend and mentor, Coach Cooks. Moments before the nurses were to wheel me away to surgery, Coach came wheeling in. I was so surprised to see him and almost embarrassed that I was so tired and still in a lot of pain. He grabbed my hand and proceeded to pray over me for the next several minutes. A deep peace filled my mind and soul, and all of my fears and pain seemed to subside. Basketball had brought us together, but it was ultimately our faith as brothers of Christ that would cement our lifelong friendship.

For the next few days after surgery, I'd lie in bed at night with extreme pain. While I was never  big believer in pain relievers, I couldn't fall asleep without my medication. After about ten days, I was off the medication completely and determined to get back to school. With two broken arms in soft casts, I had been counseled by my advisor in the College of Business to take the semester off. As much as that made sense, with everything I had been through, I wasn't mentally prepared to miss graduation with all of my classmates. Friends would carry my backpack, and I had a note taker in each class. In two short weeks, I pushed myself to start typing again. When I got sore, I'd stop, but every day I'd get a bit stronger.

In a weird and twisted situation, my Theology professor said he would allow me to type my final exam, instead of writing it out via blue book, but that I would get the same amount of time as every other student. A part of me understood his logic, but the other half told him that I simply couldn't type very fast because my arms would fatigue after only a few minutes. He didn't budge, so I sat there, fighting through the pain in a cold sweat. I finished that exam using every minute allowed. When grades were released a few days later, I saw an "A" next to my name and was so proud of myself for gutting it out.

A few weeks later, I went back to Marquette High School to start coaching again. We had a senior-laden team, led by Terry Hollins, Tim Kahle, and David Grzesiak and played tremendous basketball, highlighted by a twelve-game win streak. So much of that season, however, could be attributed to a game early in the year. We had been invited to a large tournament at Marquette University's Al McGuire Center, a place that was obviously near and dear to my heart. St. Bernard's from Minneapolis had agreed to play in the tournament because their star forward, Trevor Mbakwe, was committed to Marquette for the following season. The issue was that nobody wanted to play them. In classic Coach Cooks fashion, he let the tournament director know that we'd play anybody. With Tom Crean in the stands to watch his future forward, our guys played their absolute tails off on defense, and we led at halftime. In a great high school matchup, we lost in a tight game to a team that would go on to finish 32-1. We had only played a few games, but every guy in our locker room believed that we had a championship-caliber squad.

Following the game, several media members were gathered outside the locker room, and Coach Cooks grabbed me and instructed me to join him. For the next ten minutes or so, I stood next to him, as he fielded questions about how well we played and the stellar defensive game plan on Mbakwe. In one of the wisest coaching moves I've ever witnessed, Cooks completely flipped the script. "We got outworked, outhustled, outplayed. You can't turn the ball over like that and expect to win. We have a lot of work to do." What had seemed like a David vs. Goliath matchup suddenly made everyone question who was Goliath. Parents and players alike read those comments the next day, and they changed what everyone associated with the program came to expect from that year's team.

The kids gave me a nickname of "Wrists" for obvious reasons. The pre-practice shooting contests were out for me, but I became a better coach because I was forced to teach without demonstrating. I paid much more attention to the details of the game, such as proper floor spacing, feeding the post, and playing great pressure defense on the perimeter without fouling. Most importantly, I focused on building relationships. These were *kids*, and we so often forget that.

We went 12-2 in the Greater Metro Conference, tied for first with our conference rival, Wauwatosa East. We also went back to Indianapolis and won the Brebeuf holiday tournament, defeating the host school, 62-49, in the championship game.

Heading into the playoffs, we felt good about our chances, but we'd need to get by Milwaukee Bay View, who had arguably the best backcourt in the state in Johnny Lacy and Dwight Buycks. Buycks was apparently playing with an injury and started the first half with a wrap on his right shoulder. Taking a lead into halftime, the guys were fired up, but when I saw Buycks come out of the locker room without that shoulder wrap for the second half, I knew we'd see a different team. We battled back and forth against an incredible shot maker (in Buycks), and Marquette University and the NBA would eventually appreciate his talent for the game.

It was hard for me to see those kids lose because every single one of them had improved in my two years there. Most importantly, they respected each other and wanted to be coached. The ups and downs of a season unfortunately have to end in a single game.

As we age, sports so often become only about winning. So many losing coaches talk about how they're proud of the way the kids competed, which is such an understatement if you've stood in those coaching shoes. Months of work, early mornings and late nights, and tears of joy and dejection are a part of every journey. When you coach kids that truly care about each other and respect their coaches, coaching is such an emotional profession! Hearts can be broken in a single play, and yet all involved in the game pick each other back up and have the courage to try again. I can't think of a better way to build character.

Before the season had started, Coach Cooks had connected me to a Marquette High School alumnus named Dan Smyczek. Dan was the Public Relations Director for the Milwaukee Bucks, and given my interest in sports and business, he seemed like a good guy to get to know. I met with Dan, and he offered me an internship on his team. Essentially, my job would be focused on TV/radio set up and assisting broadcasters during every Bucks home game. Dan told me he could only pay me $6/hour but wanted to gauge my interest. *Are you kidding me?* I thought. *You're going to pay me to go to all forty-two Milwaukee Bucks home games?*

I went through some training, and Dan had me perform several jobs. Tops on the list was setting up courtside monitors for the various networks broadcasting the game. In addition, we'd set up equipment at midcourt for all the statisticians and media engineers.

I'd typically arrive about four hours before tip-off, which meant I'd get to watch guys work out before the games. Guys that don't get a lot of run during the games go through pretty strenuous workouts on gameday, but most people never see them because they're done well before anyone enters the arena. In my case, I took tremendous interest in watching assistant coaches work out young players or those rehabbing injuries. On more than a few occasions, Dan would lean over and tell me to get to work.

One hour and thirty minutes before each game, the better players would come out and get their shots up. You always knew who the die-hard fans were because they'd enter the arena just as the doors opened to get this extra hour and a half of observation. I'd watch intently as guys like Stephon Marbury, Ray Allen, and Kobe Bryant put up shots. Marbury had a funny release, which impacted his ability to shoot from range. Guys like Allen shot the ball with such a compact delivery. I should also point out that Ray's calves were probably the most ripped in the league. Skills aside, the other thing that immediately jumped out was the sheer size of these guys. Even in the broadcast booth, guys like former Chicago Bull, Will Perdue, would stroll in and remind you what seven feet looks like.

Before tip-off, the media members would gather in the media room, which always had a healthy spread of snacks and finger foods. I did my best to network because A) I would need a job in six months and B) I'd sneak in a free dinner, even if it was a soda cup full of peanuts and a hot dog.

It was about an hour before the Bucks home opener, and I was assisting another intern with the players' ticket list. Essentially, there was a separate door where players' wives, friends, and family members would enter and be checked off a list. A woman walked through the door and politely introduced herself as Steve Blake's wife. This was Steve's first season in Milwaukee, and for whatever reason, her name wasn't on our list. A bit disgruntled, she dug out her cell phone, and two minutes later, Steve Blake showed up in his warmups and said matter-of-factly, "This is my wife. She'll be at every home game for the rest of the season." And that was that. While the look on Blake's face wasn't all that pleasant, deep down, I simply thought, *Way to go Steve Blake.*

A couple months later, Dan put me on door duty again, only this time he said I would be rolling solo. The job itself was simple, but I wondered what was up because two employees always worked the door. A guy showed up with a large posse and immediately solved my only question that night, which was, "Whose first name is Usher and last name Unknown?" At about 5'7", Usher (the pop star) was much shorter than I imagined, but his entire team was very nice and fun to be around. I walked them through the back of the arena to their courtside seats, and my female co-workers setting up the media equipment all then realized why I had been tasked to go solo at the door. Later, Dan put it bluntly and explained that he knew I wouldn't freak out or act unprofessional. Winning!

The Bucks weren't a very good team during the 2006-2007 season. Andrew Bogut was hurt, and Michael Redd carried the team's scoring load. On November 11, 2006, he scored 57 points against the Utah Jazz, and I sat next to a statistician, who seemed to run out of room on his shot chart. Redd was a catch and shoot player with a quick, left-handed release. If he couldn't get a look off the catch, one or two dribbles max got him to his spot, and he'd let it go.

One player who was very underappreciated was Earl Boykins. Standing only 5'5", Earl was solid in all phases of the game. He could hit the open three and had an uncanny ability not to over penetrate. Instead of taking contested shots at the rim against seven footers, he'd pull up from fifteen feet and calmly hit shots.

The Bucks finished the 2006-2007 season with a record of 28-54, which ranked second to last in the Eastern Conference. Terry Stotts was fired towards the end of the season, and Larry Krystkowiak took over for the final eighteen games.

Earlier that season, I had emailed Larry Harris, the Bucks general manager, to see if we could meet. My dream job has always been to general manage an NBA franchise. There is something about working within a confined set of rules (salary cap, players union, etc.) and being able to strategically outwit your peers, while still being able to evaluate talent. To this day, I watch players closely and think about the value they bring to a team. In my opinion, there is an extreme amount of miscalculation on the part of NBA GM's.

Back to Larry, he politely declined, to which I responded by asking if I could come to the Cousins Center (Bucks practice facility) to watch a practice. To my surprise, he agreed, and I showed up one day with a notebook in hand and watched intently as Stotts took the team through drills. Because they had played the night before, the workout was very light and contained a lot of shooting. At the time, I wasn't impressed at all. My mind was still at Marquette, where every practice, shoot-around, or even walk-through was balls to the wall. I now realize that in an 82-game season, keeping guys fresh and motivated is so important. Like a general manager, a coach strategically makes his bets and needs to know when to push. I was grateful to Stotts for the opportunity and thanked him multiple times, along with a written thank you note.

# 22

# LIFE AFTER
# BASKETBALL

Throughout that winter, I had been applying to jobs all over the country. I really wanted to work in sports marketing, whether it be for a sports agent, apparel company, or marketing/advertising business. Despite my efforts, I couldn't seem to land an interview with any of the big companies (or small ones for that matter). Rather than get discouraged, I thought back to what Brian Lammi had told me: *You need to learn how to sell.* A few weeks later, I landed an interview with Kellogg's in Chicago. To be honest, I had no idea what I was applying for. I figured it had something to do with putting Frosted Flakes in grocery stores. The job, however, was a sales representative in foodservice, which meant that I would get a territory and focus on selling everywhere other than grocery stores: school districts, colleges, hotels, restaurants, etc. After my interview, they emailed me a list of eight cities and instructed me to rate them in order, starting with the city I'd most like to live/work. Cities like Tampa, New York, Phoenix, and Philadelphia were on the list. If you asked me how I ranked them, I don't remember, and mostly because I got a call a week later that said, "Hey John, we want to send you to Salt Lake City."

*What!* I remember thinking. Salt Lake wasn't on the list, and I had never even slightly considered living in Utah. I had just spent a week researching these great cities, dreaming about what it might be like to live in each of them, and now they wanted to send me to Salt Lake.

But, the more I thought about it, maybe Salt Lake City would be a cool place? I had skied once in my entire life in seventh grade at a small hill in central Wisconsin. I wasn't Mormon, and I didn't know a single person in the state of Utah. I called them back and said, "When do I start?"

As I thought about Utah, it suddenly occurred to me that I did know someone from Utah. In fact, I knew a very important person with connections all over the state. In a weird twist, I was re-connected to Rick Majerus, and it was almost as if he had known all along. He told me to call his former assistant and gave me her cell phone number. He also sent me several emails about the history of Salt Lake City, neighborhoods to live in, and his personal take on Park City, which he referred to as a "Little Chicago." I would later live in Park City, and it is nothing even remotely close to Chicago, as the town is a charming, seasonal ski town, nestled into the Wasatch Mountains.

Anyways, I wrote down some questions and decided to give Rick's assistant a call. "Hello," she said. After I introduced myself, she somewhat firmly asked, "Where did you get this number?" In an awkward exchange, she gave me a few pointers but kept saying things like, "I haven't talked to Rick in ten years; not sure why he'd give my number out." As I thought about what she said, I imagined Rick had a lot of relationships similar to this one: the probably thousands of people out there who he considered close friends but probably hadn't talked to in years.

I found a room for rent on Craigslist with two graduate students doing coursework at the University of Utah. Our three-bedroom place was on the north side of downtown, about a mile from the Utah Jazz arena. Tatum, the owner of the condo, was a PhD student in human genetics. Vinson, the other housemate, was a master's student in chemistry. At the end of the day, even if they were terrible people to live with, I figured I'd learn a few things. When I moved in, I only had a suitcase, as it would be another two weeks before a Kellogg-appointed moving truck would arrive with the rest of my belongings. Besides my clothes and a toothbrush, I had packed an air mattress to serve as my pseudo bed.

There was a gas station a hop, skip, and a jump down the street, and I figured that would be a good place to fill the mattress up with air. With four quarters in hand, I deposited them into the air machine. For whatever reason, the air didn't seem to be flowing from the machine correctly, and before I knew it, the machine shut off, with my air bed only half inflated. I only had one more single dollar bill, but it would get me another tank, so I walked into the gas station to get some more quarters. Standing in line waiting for change is a pain in itself, but as I glanced out the window, I couldn't believe what I was seeing: a homeless man was disconnecting the air bed from the machine.

As I started to move, he took off with the mattress down the sidewalk. "Hey!" I yelled. "That's mine!" He stopped, turned back, and yelled a bunch of things I couldn't understand before ending with, "FINE!" Clearly agitated, he wound up and slung the mattress into the road. I sprinted after it and was able to retrieve it before a car could run it over, bring it back to the gas station, and complete what I had set out to do in the first place. Day one in Salt Lake City.

My goal for living in Utah was to expand my worldview. I had skied once in my lifetime, but this was the activity of choice for Utahans, so I had to learn. I went to Snowbird to try for the first time, which was a bad idea considering Snowbird has some of the most challenging ski terrain in the United States. Oops. I pizza'd for half the day before taking a pretty rough fall and watching one of my skis slide all the way to the base of the mountain. An observer came over, asked me if I was alright, and then encouraged me to ski down on one ski. Covered in snow and wiping off my goggles, I thought, *Has this guy seen me trying to ski on two skis?* Just the thought of attempting such a thing made me laugh. I proceeded to do what any reasonable person would do: I detached my other ski and hobbled about a mile down the side of the run until I finally saw that other ski.

That Thanksgiving, I drove down in my company car to Las Vegas because I couldn't afford to fly home. I ended up staying at Hooters hotel, which was right off the strip, and paying $22/night, which was less than my Thanksgiving Day buffet at the Tropicana. I laid out by the pool, played some black jack, and worked out every morning in the fitness center. Rather than just drive six hours home on Sunday, I stopped half way at Brian Head Ski Resort in southern Utah. For three days, I had enjoyed seventy plus degree weather in Las Vegas, but Brian Head was a whiteout snowstorm! As I got out of my car to survey the conditions, I thought, *This probably isn't the best idea*. But, in the spirit of adventure, I threw my winter gear on, bought a ticket from my gambling winnings, and practiced skiing all day long. I was still a terrible skier, but I loved being out there, and by the end of the day, I thought to myself, *I can do this*. It was a legendary finish to a great trip.

My career with Kellogg's would take me all over the country, but I was always able to stay connected to the game. I felt an obligation to pass on what I had learned, and deep down, I still had this burning desire to teach the game. Shortly after moving to Salt Lake, I had reached out to several high school coaches but got no responses, which always surprised me given they were getting an email from a kid who played Division 1 college basketball and wanted to *volunteer* in their program! Going into my second year there, I decided to expand my search to elementary schools, and I got connected to a guy named Gianni Ellefson. Gianni was bald, with hoop earrings and glasses and stood about 5'9". His first questions for me had nothing to do with basketball. "Do you like red wine?" When I responded in the affirmative, I pretty much answered his second question as to whether I was Mormon. One of the most unique individuals I've ever met, Gianni ran the Catholic youth league in Salt Lake. In addition, he coached a couple teams, which seemed like a lot of work given the multiple gyms, teams, and officials he had to coordinate.

Shortly after we met, Gianni called me up and told me he had two opportunities: fifth-grade girls or third-grade boys. Let's be honest. In any other situation, I'd be getting paid to babysit. I took the boys job at St. Anne's School and had about seven players. I say about because I had one kid, Larbong, who was apparently in first grade but taller than all the other kids so they let him play up. Larbong showed up to practice one day wearing a large (and I'm talking thick) gold chain. My assistant, Matt Terry, who was a PhD student at the University of Utah, told him politely to take it off. Matt had grown up in Philadelphia and played football and run track at Ursinus College in Pennsylvania. For the next five minutes, I watched a grown man argue with a first-grader, who refused to take the chain off because it was a "gift from his dad!" We played some good basketball, but in all honesty, this was third-grade hoops. I think the kids' favorite day was the ice cream party we had at the end of the season.

I had thought about coaching those same kids in fourth grade the following season, but Gianni called one day and said, "You want to coach at East High School?" Apparently, both the freshman and sophomore boys' positions were open, and Gianni wanted to take the sophomore team if I'd take the freshman. My work schedule was flexible enough that I could swing late afternoon practices, and I had just moved to an apartment a few minutes from the high school. *Here goes nothing,* I thought.

I'd never been a part of a more diverse team in my life. I had Mexican, black, white, and Asian kids, and it seemed like none of them got along. I actually asked them at one point, "Why aren't any of you friends off the court?" We spent the first half of the season learning how to work and get along and the second half learning how to win. Our practices were two hours long, with the first hour being fundamental drills, followed by live scrimmages with the sophomores. As much as I wanted the kids to improve as basketball players, I'd ask myself every night, *Are these kids becoming better young men? Are they disciplined and respectful?* East High certainly hadn't hired me to be a life coach, but I cared about those kids more than they'll ever know.

Terrence Lord assisted both my team and Gianni's and was a physical specimen, to say the least. Terrence stood about 6'7" and probably weighed 250 lbs., with broad shoulders and an engaging personality. Like my previous experience at Marquette High School, having a guy like Terrence at practice was invaluable to my interior players. It's much easier to score against a 6'3" kid when you're going against 6'7" every day in practice.

Early in the season, we'd often have Asian tour groups stroll into the East gym and start walking across the court during the middle of practice. The High School Musical movies starring Zac Efron had been filmed there, and there were literally groups every week that would nonchalantly just start walking around the gym snapping photos. The first time it happened, I got upset and started yelling at them before another coach came over and explained the situation. My bad.

My best player struggled with academics and always seemed to be hanging around school after practice. It was against the school district's rules to give players rides home, but I knew he needed one, so I'd occasionally drive him home. This kid was fourteen years old and had tattoos up and down the inside of his forearms that read, "Game Over." When I had asked him about the tattoos, he told me they were a birthday present, and that his mother had given a neighbor a case of beer for payment. As we got to know each other, I learned that he was one of seven children, and his single mother worked night shifts. When he got home, he cooked, cleaned, and helped his siblings with their homework. His bad grades had nothing to do with his intellectual ability; he just didn't have any time to do *his* work! I'm sure similar situations happen all over America, but this was happening here, right in front of me, and I needed to do something about it. Over the next few months, I got progress reports, talked with him daily, and made sure he was getting his homework done. After a game where he struggled immensely, but more importantly couldn't seem to keep his cool, we had a frank discussion about choices. Regardless of your circumstances, I told him there were no excuses. Every day was an opportunity to chase his dreams and blaming others for his shortcomings wasn't going to be a part of his story.

On the flip side, one of my favorite players that I had the privilege to coach was Joseph Hallman. Joe came from a strong, Mormon family, played quarterback on the freshman football team, and was well-liked. What I loved about Joseph was that he got better every week, and I mean that literally. As we entered the Judge Memorial city tournament, Joseph was shooting close to 50% from three-point range, didn't force shots, and competed hard on the defensive end.

East had a star freshman named Parker Van Dyke that had been playing on the varsity. Heading into the freshman city tournament, he obviously wanted to participate with his friends, but the decision was made to hold him out. Like it or not, it would give my current team a chance to showcase their improvement. Parker had a great career at East High and would go on to play at the University of Utah.

We were a sub .500 team through the first half of the season but really picked it up in the second half. I was proud to see every guy's individual skill level improve. From guards to posts, my entire team could handle the ball and get to the basket. When players feel more comfortable with the ball and start to trust their teammates, great things happen. In our first game of the city tournament, we faced a kid named Jalen Moore, who would go on to star at Utah State and play for the Milwaukee Bucks summer league squad. A long, rangy athlete, I've seen thousands of kids play basketball, but he ranks as one of the top in terms of his feel for the game at such a young age. Physically overmatched, we lost to a better team.

Fortunately, for us, the tournament was double elimination, and we'd have a chance to play our way back into contention. For the next three games, we played the best basketball of our season and won third place, beating a team that we wouldn't have competed with earlier in the year. After that victory, I walked into the locker room and was doused with a Gatorade bucket, the only time in my life. That game, season, and overall experience meant a lot to those kids, and it certainly meant something to me.

I spent that spring traveling all over the states of Utah, Idaho, Colorado, Nevada, and Wyoming for work. During every trip, I made a point to do things that took me out of my comfort zone. After a long day of meetings in Moab, I changed clothes in my car and ran through Arches National Park until the sun set. The next night, I toured the famous Hole N"The Rock house, a 5,000-square-foot abode built into the side of a mountain. While the house was impressive, I couldn't get over the taxidermied horse that greeted visitors in the living room. I've seen a lot of mounts before, but the horse was kind of creepy.

Being on the road so much made it imperative that I take care of my body, but I told myself early on that hotel fitness centers would take a back seat if there was something better to see outside. I ran through the orange and pink landscape of Flaming Gorge, ran through the ghost casino town of Wendover, NV, and even found myself in Dinosaur, CO, where the Dinosaur National Monument is known locally as "The Little Grand Canyon." I'd visit Bryce, Zion, and Capitol Reef National Parks and hike the famous Angel's Landing. In Idaho, I spent time exploring the Snake River and jogging the amazing bridges in Twin Falls. In Page, AZ, I hiked the legendary slot canyons of Antelope Canyon, accompanied by a Native American tour guide named Barry. I saw things that amazed me, met people that challenged the way I saw the world, and couldn't help but stop on multiple occasions to admire the spectacular work of God's creation.

I was a sales rep making $38,000/year, and yet, I got more out of life because I wasn't afraid of the unknown. If I learned one thing from Scott and Coach Crean, it's that you can't be afraid of what you're capable of. I was literally taking the "Maximize the Day" concept and applying it to my life.

Late in August, I checked into a hotel in Jackson Hole, WY. "Welcome Mr. Willkom," said a cheerful woman at the front desk. "We see that you'll be staying with us for the next four nights, is that correct?" "Why yes, it is!" I told her. She proceeded to explain that the resort had just finished building some condo units that would go up for sale in the next month or two. Rather than stick me in the hotel, she smiled and said, "Enjoy one of our four-bedroom condos for the week!"

As I walked through the front door, a nice fruit basket awaited me on the kitchen table, along with a note encouraging me to explore a "life in Jackson Hole." "Starting at $1.3 million" was written in fine print below that.

The condo had two balconies, each with a hot tub on it. Every night after work, I'd take a run along the Snake River and watch fly fishermen stand along the banks, illuminated by a golden sunset. On Wednesday, I tried a beer called "Bitch Creek" at the Million Dollar Cowboy bar and sat on a saddle-like bar stool as I watched the locals line dance. One after another, men would walk in sporting large belt buckles, tucked in collared shirts, and cowboy hats. This wasn't some kind of show, but a way of life for those that lived there.

For the next four nights, I'd lie down in a different bed (had to put that four-bedroom condo to use)! I thought about the beautiful memories I had created during my time on the road. For all of the sales meetings, presentations, and negotations that had been responsible for those trips, I knew it would be everything outside of work that I'd ultimately remember.

# 23

# MAD DOG

I had managed to make a few friends in Salt Lake, and one of them had invited me down to BYU to play flag football. After playing for about thirty minutes, I kept wondering why these guys weren't throwing me the ball. "I'm wide open on almost every play," I told them. Our quarterback responded, "You're running all of the wrong routes." "Excuse me" is what I meant to say, but I responded with a confused look and simply said, "What?"

"We're getting ready for our fall flag football league, and you're not running any of the plays that we've practiced." I couldn't help but laugh. Not only was I not a student, but I had never met any of these guys before. *Why on earth would I know their plays? Why would I know that they had plays?* I was there to play football and break a sweat!

Obviously frustrated, I told them I'd catch up with them another time, and I left. I had quite a bit of steam yet to burn, so I swung by a 24 Hour Fitness in Provo and walked into the basketball gym. There was only one guy in there, and immediately I knew who it was. Mark "Mad Dog" Madsen had been a standout at Stanford and led them to the final four in 1998. At 6'9", 245 lbs., he was an intimidator down low and developed a reputation for his grit and tenacity. He would later win two NBA championships with the Shaq & Kobe Lakers in 2001 and 2002. Shaq would go on to say that he was the only man that could physically compete with him: "He used to beat me up in practice" (Rohlin).

*What the hell was Mark Madsen doing in Provo, UT?* At the same time, having been around Marquette and the Bucks, the last thing I wanted to do was bug a guy who was trying to work out. So, I worked out on one side, and he did his thing on the other. After about forty-five minutes, he came over and asked if I wanted to do some drills together. We worked on perimeter/post entries, partner shooting, and a variety of other drills. It was great. At the end, we chatted for a while, and I just asked him, "Why Provo?" He told me that he was Mormon, single, and that he figured this was the best place to meet a wife in the offseason. Made complete sense to me. Before he left, he told me to look him up on Facebook and to send him a message if I wanted to come to a game. At the time, he was playing for the Minnesota Timberwolves, and knowing that they'd come to Salt Lake once probably several months down the road, I thanked him, knowing I'd never see him again.

Back in Salt Lake, I had a neighbor that was a cook at Chipotle. This guy stood about 5'6", with a scraggly, black beard and always wore a hat. He was in his late thirties, loved sports, and would stand outside his apartment smoking cigarettes and reading the sports section of the Salt Lake Tribune. Because of my job in outside sales, I'd go back and forth from my apartment several times a day, so I'd often catch him outside having a smoke. He had a young daughter and was doing his best to make ends meet, but he worked a lot of hours and had dreams to work at a trendy restaurant. While better pay and hours seemed to be his short-term issues, the guy believed he had the skills to be a top chef. Every day during basketball season, I'd stop and chat for a few minutes, and he'd always ask if the Jazz were going to win that night. He had never been to a game and talked about how cool it would be to go. "I just want to see those guys up close and hear them yell at the officials!" he said.

One day as I was leaving for work, his head popped out from behind the newspaper. "The T'wolves are in town tonight. Who you got?" My mind immediately went to Madsen, and then I thought, *There's no way he remembers me.* "The Jazz are a better team," I told him.

All morning, I kept thinking about reaching out to Mad Dog. The chances of him responding were slim, but I eventually concluded that it didn't matter. Between meetings that day, I sent Mark Madsen a Facebook message, and not thirty minutes later, he responded and said, "How many tickets do you want?"

I came home from work that night, and my neighbor just happened to be outside, smoking a cigarette and reading the paper. "The T'wolves are really improved, and the Jazz have been struggling," I blurted out as I walked up the stairs. "What!" he responded. My comments seemed to agitate him, as he fumbled the paper to the side of his body so he could see me, while firmly gripping his cigarette. "The Jazz need this one at home; you can't say that," he responded shaking his head.

"Well, they're going to need your support. You want to go to the game?" His face lit up, as if he had just been invited to Disney World. "Tonight's game? But it starts in a couple hours?" he questioned. "Yes, we're leaving in an hour," I told him. "I'll need to check with my wife," he said. "Well, check right now," I told him. He awkwardly stumbled into his apartment, holding his newspaper, and then slipped back outside the door. "What time are we leaving?"

Madsen had gone out of his way. Our tickets were at center court, about ten rows up. He came over before the game and said "hello" to my neighbor and I. Mark Madsen will never read this, but he made my neighbor's year that night. I know that because I must've heard every detail from that game for the next six months. And the Jazz did beat the T'wolves.

I played quite a bit of basketball myself during my time in Salt Lake. Initially, I was playing in a pretty competitive league at a local Mormon temple gym on Wednesday nights. Most of the temples had gyms, and this particular league had several former college players from places like BYU and Utah State. It wasn't so organized that we had referees, but guys played hard, and winners always stayed.

At the Division 1 level, you become adept at initiating contact every time you drive the lane. In high school, I'd drive to score. In college, you're coached to drive into the defense: create contact and force the official to make a call. Once you feel the contact, you focus on making the shot. Playing this way in pick-up basketball is admittedly frowned upon, and it takes a concerted effort to go back to your old ways and not launch yourself into people when driving to the basket.

One Wednesday, I was driving to the rim, and before I could even leave my feet, a former Utah State player shoved me out of bounds. This wasn't a "basketball play," but a blatant two-handed shove in the back that sent me sprawling to the ground. This guy stood about 6'10" and had been talking trash all night, probably because his team was losing by a healthy margin. I didn't respond kindly to that shove and was actually asked to leave for "swearing." While I had several positive experiences with people of the Mormon faith, it was often very hypocritical when guys would play dirty but point fingers when it came to language.

On a more positive note, my friend Kevin Albers and I drove to Park City on a Saturday to go to one of our favorite bars, O'Shucks. O'Shucks was a Park City staple, serving 40 oz. schooners of beer and offering free peanuts to its patrons. Like a typical Saturday night, the bar was packed, so we proceeded to the back to see if we could snag a table or booth. No dice. As we scanned the room, Kevin turned to me and said, "Hey, is that Aaron Rodgers?" Before I could think as to why Green Bay Packers quarterback, Aaron Rodgers, would be in a random Utah Irish pub on a Saturday night, I looked to my left and sure enough. Sitting in a half circle booth, Rodgers was wearing a blue dress shirt and charcoal-colored sport coat. Kevin and I both agreed that we'd say hi to him but didn't want to interrupt his night, so we did exactly that. After introducing ourselves and telling him we were from Wisconsin, to our surprise, he got out of the booth and wanted to continue the conversation. He explained that he was there to meet some college friends from Cal before flying to Hawaii for the Pro Bowl. The Packers had just lost in the Playoffs to Arizona in a 51-45 overtime thriller the previous weekend. Before we could leave, he looked at me and said, "Do you want to play me in Buck Hunter?" Growing up hunting in Wisconsin, I was up for the challenge, and we each took our shots. Rodgers is certainly a better quarterback than a gamer. He shook my hand, posed for a photo with Kevin and I, and wished us well before walking out of the bar.

Since Rodgers and the boys had vacated the booth, we took over, and about ten minutes later, a waitress showed up and proceeded to put down ten pitchers of beer on the table in front of us. After the first couple, I looked at her, somewhat concerned, and said, "Excuse me, but we didn't order these." She smiled and said, "That guy in the suit coat ordered you guys ten pitchers of beer." For the next hour or so, we walked around and filled everyone's glass in the back of the bar, courtesy of the Packers quarterback. Love him or hate him, I will always be a fan of Aaron Rodgers.

# 24

# STAY CONNECTED TO THE GAME

I had spent three and a half years in Utah, the last in which I was honored with a Golden K award, given to the best Kellogg's salesperson in the country in each channel. As part of the awards ceremony, I was asked to give a speech at the national sales meeting in Orlando, FL. Standing behind the stage, I could see the bright lights and thousands of people sitting in the ballroom. I admittedly had butterflies in my stomach, and I thought, *What if I blow this?* But then I told myself, *You were built to be able to do this. You've played in front of thousands of hostile fans and been pushed to the absolute edge of failure. You're prepared and deserve to be here. Go up there and act like you're the best salesperson in the country.* I closed my eyes, took a deep breath, and walked out to a standing ovation as my name was announced.

A couple months after my speech, Kellogg's promoted me to a larger market in southern California, and I found a room for rent in a three-bedroom house, one block from the sand on Newport Beach's Balboa Peninsula. My friends kept telling me to get a nicer place inland, but I wanted the California experience, and in my mind, that meant being as close to the beach as possible. Despite the Craigslist horror stories, I had used the platform to great success in Utah and found my place in Newport on there as well!

Living in California was amazing. I played basketball on an outdoor court almost every day, ran along the beach, and even bought a road bike to explore the coast. I also made it a point to jump in the ocean every day. For a year straight, I went into that ocean, even if it was only for a minute. I'm sure a lot of native Californians thought I was crazy, but what's wrong with appreciating what's around you?

Once I got my bearings in Newport, I started coaching for the Newport Lightning Basketball Club. We had players from all over Orange County and had coaches in the program like Jeff Fryer, the former Loyola Marymount sharpshooter who famously teamed with Hank Gathers and Bo Kimble. What I really enjoyed about the Lightning was that I would run skill clinics twice a week for multiple ages. In short, I didn't coach a single team but would work out one night with fifth-graders and another night with high school kids.

I would later coach the ninth and tenth-graders in a few tournaments because they needed a coach. In all my years of basketball, there was a stark difference in the work ethics of these kids in the OC vs. everywhere else I had coached. Kids just didn't care as much. Seems harsh, I know. The little kids were great and truly made the experience enjoyable because they were so eager to learn and get better. The older kids, though, just had such a false sense of hard work. I'd watch guys go half speed, miss crazy-looking finger rolls around the basket, and shoot thirty-five-foot three-point shots. Any constructive feedback would elicit looks of disgust, as if, *Is this guy really saying this stuff to me?* We lost a tournament game to the highly-touted Compton Magic by more than forty points, and every guy on the team walked off the court smiling and joking around. I was downright embarrassed, not by the loss itself, but because nothing in those kids' souls prompted any visible display of a setback, disappointment, or regret. It was hard to associate myself with that type of effort.

I thought back to one of the Playmakers teams I had coached

several years earlier. I had taken over a seventh-grade team that had lost to the Wisconsin Playground Warriors by forty-six points two weeks before. I knew I needed to whip these guys into shape, but more importantly, had to teach them how to compete. We would go on to play the Playground Warriors again, and we not only competed, but we beat them. Duane Wilson Sr., who coached his son Duane Wilson on that team, complained to the tournament directors about the officiating after the game. "We beat them fair & square," I told the directors, as I walked out of a raucous gym. I had strategically thrown a handful of rotating defensive looks at them, going from zone defenses to box and ones and triangle and twos. In a nutshell, I wanted to force their best players to think. When great athletes all of a sudden have to think, occasionally you can get them to stop being great players. On the flip side, my guys felt they had a competitive advantage (and they had also worked their butts off for two weeks), which led to a renewed confidence. Duane Wilson would play at Marquette and Texas A&M years later, but I know the kids on that Playmakers team will never forget that game.

My point in comparing the Newport and Playmakers teams is that the latter cared enough to learn how to win. If you don't care, you don't improve, and people that don't improve rarely win consistently.

That summer, I met my childhood friend and Playmakers co-founder, Mike Lee, in Las Vegas for NBA Summer League. During the first day of games, I was sitting about half way up the bleachers, and Mark Cuban walked up and sat down right next to me. "Who's your team?" he blurted out, with a big grin on his face. "I'm a Milwaukee Bucks fan," I told him with a smile. "I love the city of Milwaukee," he responded. We chatted for a bit, and I asked him about his interest in buying the Chicago Cubs. "You think if somebody offers you $800 million, they would return a phone call," he said.

Later that day, I noticed a man with wiry, gray hair sitting courtside, a few rows in front of me. He stood out like a sore thumb because of his outfit, which consisted of a pink, Nike tennis hat, a pink shirt, and pink socks and shoes to match. It was quite a look. I asked a few people near me, "Who is that guy?" One guy finally replied, "Oh him, that's Jimmy Goldstein."

I pulled out my phone, and sure enough, that was him. But who was Jimmy Goldstein, and why was he sitting courtside wearing such crazy clothes? I'd go on to learn that James Goldstein was an NBA super fan that attended more than a hundred games each year. In fact, he not only attended, but he'd sit courtside at every game, wearing the craziest of outfits. When the NBA season would end, he'd travel the world attending fashion shows. No one really knew how James accumulated his wealth, but his mantra of "basketball, fashion, and architecture" had made him somewhat of an icon.

I walked up to James Goldstein after the game, introduced myself, and then asked him the same question Cuban asked me, "Who are you rooting for?"

"I just love watching NBA basketball," he told me and then proceeded to advise me to look him up in Los Angeles, which subtly meant, *I have to go.*

The next year for my birthday in May, my girlfriend at the time actually tried to arrange a lunch meeting with me and James Goldstein in Los Angeles. While he declined the lunch, he sent me a signed 8x10 photo of him wearing a snakeskin leather hat, jacket, and pants. I wasn't quite sure what I was supposed to do with it, as it's not every day you receive a framed picture of a male model in his seventies wearing all leather!

I displayed the picture on a bookshelf in my living room, and it has been the number one conversation starter when guests come to my house.

In addition to the summer league games, Mike and I were interested in a visit to Impact Basketball, led by legendary NBA skills trainer Joe Abunassar. Drew Moore, one of Joe's skills trainers, agreed to let us come observe a workout. The first thing that strikes you at Impact is the amount of training tools available. In addition to the basketball side of things, they have everything a player could ever want to maximize their ability: body composition analysis, media training, food & nutrition consulting, and much more. I watched Brooke Lopez warm up, and several other NBA players proceeded to walk in. The workout itself was great, and Drew, in the politest way possible, reminded me, "No pictures."

At Impact, guys would come in all day long, and skills trainers were available to work them out. I can't verify this, but I had heard that NBA players paid a monthly membership and could come as often as they liked. Guys training to secure a roster spot may work out three times a day, followed by open run in the evenings. Seasoned veterans would buy a membership, alert their team that they were working out at Impact for the summer, and then proceed to show up once or twice a month, while enjoying the rest of what Las Vegas had to offer.

Going to Las Vegas was kind of a last hurrah for me, as I would begin the pursuit of my MBA in about a month. Going back to graduate school was a goal of mine, and after months of studying for the GMAT and applying to schools, I decided on Loyola Marymount. Marymount was another Jesuit school like Marquette, and I'd be taking classes from 6-9 p.m. in the evenings, while continuing to work full time. My first semester schedule was a mix of finance, business law, and accounting, as I signed up for subjects that were outside of what I knew, figuring that my dollars would be better spent actually learning something than getting straight "A's" in sales and marketing classes. Loyola was in Marina del Rey, just south of Los Angeles, and I knew I'd need to move out of Newport Beach. In one year, I had made so many great friends, but growth often takes you out of your comfort zone.

In the summer of 2011, I moved into a four-bedroom house in Manhattan Beach, CA. The move itself got off to a bit of a rough start. As I pulled up the U-Haul, I heard a loud grinding sound and immediately stopped the truck. When I jumped out, I could see that I had wedged the truck against an overhang that protruded over the driveway from another house in front of ours. Long story short, I knocked on the door of that house, showed them what happened, and later got a hefty bill for the damage. I guess doing the right thing can be expensive sometimes.

I had two female housemates, a bartender and a wine rep, and a male housemate named Donny DeBruno. Donny was in his mid-thirties and about 5'5", with jet black curly hair. During the day, Donny worked as a manager at REI in Santa Monica but at night would come home and design skateboard display racks out of wood in our garage. The name of his business? Double D Racks! As I got to know Donny, his business seemed to be doing quite well, as his displays were all over southern California surf and skate shops, and he was working on taking his production overseas. Donny was also doing additional promotional work, which included screen-printed apparel featuring the Double D Racks logo. If you're ever in need of a unique Christmas gift for a special female in your life, Double D was even selling logoed thongs due to "high customer demand."

I lived with Donny and the crew for a year and then was approached with an opportunity to move to Chicago to work at Kellogg's Specialty Channels corporate headquarters. It was a big promotion for me, but it meant another new home, new friends, and a new basketball family. After two more years of graduate school and working full time, I finished my MBA at Loyola Chicago (where I had been able to transfer all of my credits from Loyola Marymount). It was a bittersweet moment for me, because while I felt accomplished, I was so burnt out from the late nights and early mornings. For two years, I'd show up to work on little to no sleep and do my best. I took my last final exam on a Tuesday night in February. Walking out of Loyola's Quinlan School of Business in downtown, the cold, Chicago air filled my lungs, and snow fell from the sky, glowing in the bright city lights. I literally took a moment just to stop, look around, and reflect on all of it.

As I stood on that street corner, I closed my eyes and thought about my life up to that point. Similar to my experience at Marquette, getting my MBA was about proving to myself that I could do it. I thought back to Jack Bennett's speech, which constantly begged the question: Do you have the abilities needed to succeed?

For the last time, I'd ride the "L" train back home and have to empty the used, Ziploc sandwich bags from my backpack. The late-night study sessions were over, and there would be no more required text book reading on flights to and from business clients. And yet, my actual degree meant very little to me compared to the journey that I had taken to get there. My drive, discipline, and will to win ultimately carried me through. This wasn't the end; it was the beginning of a new chapter, with a renewed spirit for lifelong learning. Before I could think about what would be next, I walked into my apartment and went straight to bed. Mission accomplished.

I spent the next few months living life like a normal person. For the first time in three years, I felt like I had free time. Justin Zimmer and Paul Clevenstine were my two best friends in the city, and we went on several "groupers," which were basically three on three dates. On Saturdays, Paul would often get me into the East Bank Club, which is the premier gym in downtown Chicago. Even referring to this place as a gym is an understatement, as it has an indoor driving range, rooftop pool & bar, steakhouse, multiple cafes, tennis courts, and more. It was a country club on steroids, but none the less, a day pass was often a literal day rotating between activities.

The next fall, I had the itch again to get back into coaching, and a priest at the church I attended put me in touch with the school's athletic director. After exchanging a few emails, we sat down one day, and I left that meeting as the new fourth-grade boys' basketball coach at Old St. Mary's School in the South Loop of the city. We practiced twice a week at the De La Salle girls' campus and spent 90% of our time working on fundamentals. I remember the cold nights walking into that dark gym and thinking to myself, *This reminds me of my dad's practices in St. John's gym when I was a little kid.* Every Saturday, we'd play at a different school in the Chicago Catholic League. Many of the gyms were old, the floors dirty, and the bleachers worn-down. Little kids would be selling popcorn and candy at mock concession stands, and adult volunteers charged everyone $1 for a "ticket." Often, I'd help kids figure out the game clock or teach them how to use the official scorebook. Basketball was why we were there, but I admittedly stopped on several occassions and thought, *This is so much more than just a game.* Every game had a few tears, as well as new experiences: kids making their first shots, taking a charge, or getting a steal.

For thirty years, I had been around this game, but these little kids brought tremendous joy to my life. For the first time, I honestly didn't care about the score. Each week, I'd teach something new, and then we'd go back to basics. Basketball is a game that needs to be taught, and while I had just finished being a student for three years, my greater purpose in life to teach was highlighted with these kids. We'd run "man makers," and I'd have the guys in a defensive stance until their legs shook (max like thirty seconds), and then we'd take a charge and scream so the city of Chicago could hear us. Pride knows no boundaries.

We finished the season by participating in the Catholic League City Tournament. In our second game, we faced a team that had blown us out earlier in the season. Led by a kid named "Richard," who everyone on my team seemed to know, we got down early and were down by ten points in the fourth quarter. Now, ten points in fourth-grade basketball is the equivalent of about thirty in the NBA. When games are played in the teens and twenties, it's basically game over. Miraculously, we got a couple buckets and then in a chaotic last minute of the game, we forced multiple steals that turned into layups. Walking out of that gym 36-34 victors and seeing the kids mobbed by the hundreds of spectators was pretty special.

On June 14, 2014, Paul, Justin, and I attended the Old Town Art Fest, which is a summer festival in one of my favorite Chicago neighborhoods. If you've ever been to Chicago in the summer time, the city is legendary for its street fests. There is literally a different fest every weekend from Memorial Day to Labor Day. Each fest claims a cultural heritage or positive cause, but let's be honest: people show up to drink, listen to live music, and eat fried foods in the street! After walking around the fest for a couple hours, my friends and I headed into Pour House bar to meet some buddies for dinner. We all grabbed a burger and a beer and threw out ideas for what we should do next. I had a hard time joining the conversation because I kept staring at this girl.

She was with a group of her friends near the bar and was wearing a pink shirt. I could tell she was younger than me, and at every glance, I thought, *Wow, she's beautiful.* I'm not sure what convinced me to finally go talk to her, but I walked over and said "hello," and we started a conversation that would last four hours. Allison was her name, and ironically, she had grown up in Newport Beach, CA, attended Duke as an undergrad, and was in medical school for podiatry at Rosalind Franklin University in North Chicago.

A few days later, I took the train forty-five minutes north to meet Allison for our first date at Spacca Napoli, a fancy pizza place in her Ravenswood neighborhood. We laughed and talked so much that we each had a box of pizza to take home for leftovers. Holding the pizza boxes on the corner, we awkwardly hugged, but I remember thinking to myself that I had never felt more at ease on a first date.

Our second date was a five-mile run in ninety plus degree weather. Allison ran the whole way in a long sleeve jacket, but she laughed and chatted the entire time, and I still smile thinking about it. I learned that Allison had been one of the top distance runners as a prep in California, who was heavily recruited before ultimately choosing Duke. As she talked about her past and the hard work and discipline that seemed to weave its way into every story, I couldn't help but think about how similarly we viewed our lives.

Fast forward to the fall, and I took some clients to the Packers/Bears game. In true Green Bay fashion, the Packers dismantled the Bears, but I don't remember the game at all because later that day, I told Allison I loved her for the first time. She was so happy and so was I. It was such a great moment.

For the next year, Allison spent five months in various cities on podiatry rotations, and we worked hard to build our relationship, despite being so far apart. I looked forward to the times I could visit and tried not to think about the times that I couldn't. I got a Southwest Airlines credit card and used my mileage to fly to Denver, Boston, San Francisco, Portland, and San Diego. Long distance is never easy, but you learn a lot about a person's character when the going gets tough, and our commitment to each other never wavered.

On February 20, 2016, my Old St. Mary's fifth-grade basketball team played their butts off, and we won a close game in Chicago's north side. After the game, I was chatting with a set of parents in the parking lot. "What are you up to this weekend?" they asked.

"Well," I said. "I'm actually going to ask Allison to marry me tonight." They were so excited for me and promised not to tell anyone, to which we all laughed.

I had been painting a canvas in my bedroom for three weeks. "What?" you might ask. I had decided to paint Allison a picture of the Chicago skyline, along with the lakefront path that we ran several times a week. In large, white letters, the phrase, "Will you marry me," jumped off the canvas.

Allison had wanted to come over several times in that three-week period, and at one point expressed her frustration, "You never want me to come over anymore!" I felt bad; I really did. But, I had to finish that painting!

Allison had asked me several times if we could go to a "wine & paint" night. There was a place in our neighborhood called Bottle & Bottega, and I called them and explained my plan. I wanted to attend a class on a Saturday night and then take Allison over to the "paintings for sale" after we were done. We had been looking for some artwork to jazz my place up a bit, so she wouldn't balk at that suggestion. From there, I'd have her flip through the paintings until she got to mine, when I would then propose to her.

I sat through that painting class for two hours, nervously checking my pocket every few minutes to make sure the ring was still there. We painted pictures of this funky tree/sunset scene, and our two canvases looked completely different! When the class ended, I walked her over to the bin of paintings, and we went through each one, starting from the beginning. I wasn't sure where the girl at the front desk had placed my painting, but after about four, I knew it had to be up soon.

When she finally pulled that painting out, I dropped to a knee and said everything that I wanted to say. Leading up to that, I had thought about the myriad of life experiences we had shared, the months of long distance, and how I had randomly met a beautiful track star turned doctor eating cheeseburgers with my friends. I thought about the man I had become: how basketball had almost served as a metaphor to the love and commitment that was ultimately built for her. Friends of mine complain about their wives and the boredom of marriage, but I can honestly say I found my soulmate, which makes all the difference.

Around the same time, we found out that Allison had matched for her residency program in Portland, OR. Thirty hours from Chicago, we'd both moved around the country before, but this would be different because we'd be doing it together.

We got married on April 22, 2017, in Newport Beach, CA, at Allison's home parish, which was important to us given our mutual Catholic faith. My two brothers were my best men and rapped their reception speech to a custom version of Bruno Mars', "That's What I Like," which probably shocked most of Allison's extended family but came as no surprise to me, given their creative personalities. People came from all over the country, including my high school coach, Gordie Sisson, and of course, Coach Cooks. It was the perfect day, surrounded by the people we love. God is good.

# 2 5

# REFLECTION

"Bang!" I almost jump out of my seat as the airplane touches down. "Are you ok?" says the woman sitting next to me. "Um yeah, yeah, I'm good," I tell her. "I've never seen anyone sleep through an entire plane ride," she tells me. "You didn't even wake up during all of the announcements about landing!"

*Thanks*? I thought to myself. Still half in a daze, I myself couldn't believe that I had just slept for five straight hours. And not waking up at all during the descent? Wow, that was a serious dream. But what a dream it was.

As I walk off the plane, I'm greeted by our CEO, who immediately goes into full business mode, rattling off facts and figures that all seem so insignificant. I smile and nod as we walk towards the rental car area of the airport.

"I was having some issues with the wi-fi, were you? he asks.

Still reflecting on my dream, I offer a somewhat delayed, "Um, not really."

Over the next two days, I present to a group of impressive business partners in New York. All of my preparation is rewarded, and I'm proud of what I accomplish.

As I board the plane back to Portland (in a window seat this time), I can't help but reflect on a life so consumed by basketball. Would my life have been different if Kevin Orr wasn't my gym teacher in first grade? What if Noel Dartt never got in that car accident, or if

Joe Konieczny had chosen not to coach a group of seventh grade kids that he had never met? What if Dave MacArthur would've said "no thanks" to the idea of starting a basketball camp? What did Tom Crean, Coach Cooks, and Rick Majerus see in me that I didn't? I was unbelievably blessed to be around men of tremendous character, who ultimately chose to share their love of the game with me. And although I spent twenty-one years trying to perfect my skills as a player, I think those guys knew that they were ultimately preparing me for where I am right now.

I'm a respectful, honest, and hard-working man that loves to compete. Every day, I'm either getting better or getting worse. I never stay the same. And while Joe Konieczny used to yell, "Ten more seconds," it's that extra push, that devotion to discipline when everyone else wants to quit, that drives me. I haven't taken a jump shot lately, but I have fourteen employees that depend on me every day, and you better believe that I'm prepared to lead them.

I call my wife when I land, and in a pleasant surprise, she tells me to hustle home because she got us Trail Blazers tickets for tonight's game. Tom Crean used to tell me, "Find a way to stay connected to the game." A couple beers, my wife, and a Blazers win sums up the perfect evening. As we proceed towards the exit doors of the arena, a tall man directs the crowds. We make eye contact, and a big smile crosses his face. Terrence Lord had assisted me in Salt Lake City at East High School and was now helping out at Blazers games in the evenings to "stay connected to the game." After some laughs and a rundown of each other's lives, a somewhat concerned look crosses his face. "Are you coaching?" he asks. "No, I just haven't had time since I moved to Portland. New job, new wife, new apartment; maybe one of these days." And even as I almost strategically try to convince myself that I just don't have time for basketball, the smile on his face slowly fades and his lips firm up. "Ya know, my son is playing in a new AAU program, and they need a new coach."

# WORKS CITED

Associated Press. "MAN MAY HAVE DIED FROM ASPIRATING SODA." *Madison.com*, 6 December. 2006,
http://host.madison.com/news/local/man-may-have-died-from-aspirating-soda/article_01c9e10d-f521-545f-ba68-24f68c79a0f9.html. Accessed 25 Feb 2018.

Rohlin, Melissa. "Shaquille O'Neal says Kobe Bryant among greatest ever." *LA Times,* 30 November 2011, http://lakersblog.latimes.com/lakersblog/2011/11/shaq-shaquille-oneal-kobe-bryant-.html

Roquemore, Bobbi. "Coach Doesn't Change Direction." *Milwaukee Journal Sentinel*, 17 December. 2003, http://www.takeittotherim.com/news_1.htm

Rutherford, Mike. "The Eight Most Memorable Louisville/Marquette Games of Recent Memory." *Card Chronicle*, 17 Februrary 2007, https://www.cardchronicle.com/2007/2/17/122857/089. Accessed 25 Feb 2018.

The Life and Times of Rick Majerus. (2008, January 16). *Sports Illustrated*. Retrieved from
https://www.si.com/college-basketball/2008/01/16/majerus0121

Made in the USA
Monee, IL
15 June 2021

71282269R00121